Evaluating and Selecting
EFL Teaching Materials

Alan Cunningsworth

With *A Glossary of Basic EFL Terms*
by Brian Tomlinson

HEINEMANN EDUCATIONAL BOOKS
LONDON

Heinemann Educational Books Ltd
22 Bedford Square, London WC1B 3HH

LONDON   EDINBURGH   MELBOURNE   AUCKLAND
HONG KONG   SINGAPORE   KUALA LUMPUR
NEW DELHI   IBADAN   NAIROBI   JOHANNESBURG
EXETER (NH)   KINGSTON   PORT OF SPAIN

ISBN 0 435 28006 6

🅑🅛 British Library Cataloguing in Publication Data

Cunningsworth, Alan
Evaluating and selecting EFL teaching materials.
1. English language--study and teaching—Foreign
speakers   2. Teaching—aids and devices
I. Title   II. Tomlinson, Brian
428.2′4′07   PE1128.A2

ISBN 0–0435–28006–6

Phototypesetting by Georgia Origination, Liverpool.
Printed in Great Britain by Biddles Ltd, Guildford.

Contents

Preface

The aim of this book is to put forward and discuss in a practical fashion some ideas on how to analyse EFL coursebooks and other teaching materials in a systematic and meaningful way. Such an analysis is a useful tool in evaluating the potential of a coursebook when matched against the learning objectives of those who might use it. It is also possible to evaluate course material in general terms, without reference to a specific group of learners, by using generally accepted principles of language teaching as a basis for evaluation. In many cases however, teachers will wish to evaluate more specifically, having a particular type of learner, or even a definite class, in mind. This book is intended to help the teacher, and course director, with both general and specific evaluation.

Four basic principles for evaluating ELF teaching materials are outlined in the introductory Chapter 1 and an example is given of how to use these principles in practice. My aim in Chapters 2 to 8 is to discuss from a number of different perspectives the criteria which will assist us in a detailed analysis of course materials and which will help us to build up as full a picture as possible of the material which we wish to evaluate. Each of these chapters represents a different perspective, focusing on one aspect of analysis and evaluation. There is also a progression from one chapter to the next. We begin with an analysis of the kind of English being presented by the teaching material (the language content) and develop through consideration of selection and grading, teaching methodology and testing procedures to factors directly connected with the psychology of the student and his approach to learning. So we begin by looking at what is being taught (the language content) and then go on to consider how it is taught, and finish by relating these perspectives to the psychology of the learner. In Chapter 9 there are some practical suggestions for adapting and extending course book activities.

The criteria for evaluation which are discussed in Chapters 2 to 8, are reproduced in Chapter 10 in the form of an easy-reference checklist of questions we must ask ourselves about a coursebook in order to build up a picture of its potential use and value.

I am not aware of any book in the field of English language teaching which attempts to deal with materials evaluation in detail, and the present book, deriving largely from work done with students on teacher-training courses over a number of years, is intended to go some way towards filling the gap.

When dealing with this subject, one inevitably embraces a wide field of study including needs analysis, syllabus design, the methodology of teaching, theories of learning and the theory and practice of testing. In an effort to be as comprehensive as possible within the limits of a short book, I have on occasion dealt with certain areas somewhat briefly rather than omit them altogether. I hope that the references in the text together with the bibliography will provide suggestions for further reading where the reader wishes to go more deeply into a particular topic.

AJC
March 1983

Abbreviations and terminology

A Glossary of Basic EFL Terms is provided on pages 80 to 102. This includes the terminology used in this book but also covers other terms that readers may come across in their studies or work in teaching English as a foreign language.

These abbreviations are used in the text and expanded in the glossary:

EFL   English as a foreign language
ESP   English for special purposes
TEFL Teaching English as a foreign language
L1   first language (mother tongue, native language)
L2   language being learned

Where the words *he*, *his* etc. are used in the text in a general sense, they are not intended to discriminate or distinguish in terms of sex, and should be read as meaning *he* or *she*, *his* or *her*, etc.

Acknowledgements

I wish to acknowledge the great debt which I owe to my students over a period of years, during which time they have made valuable comments and suggestions on procedures to be used in materials evaluation and have helped me to develop and refine the criteria put forward in this book.

The author and publishers wish to thank the following for permission to reproduce their materials and for providing illustrations:

Heinemann Educational Books Ltd – pp. 3, 4, 7, 8, 9, 10, 11, 12, 44, 54; Blond and Briggs – p. 10; Longman Group Ltd – pp. 3, 4, 27, 28, 50, 53, 66–67, 71; Edward Arnold – pp. 3, 16–17, 51; Oxford University Press – pp. 4, 27, 69; Macmillan – pp. 4, 47–48; Penguin Books Ltd – pp. 38–39, 45; Nathan Jeux – pp. 36, 37.

1 Coursebooks and Language Learning

1 Teachers and coursebooks

Most teachers of English use a coursebook. Some may use one coursebook only, taking their students through it from beginning to end, whilst others, who perhaps have more freedom and are happier when creating their own teaching programme, will take texts and exercises from several different books, adapting them where necessary and supplementing them with original material they have produced themselves. It is rare however to meet a teacher who does not to a greater or lesser extent draw on published teaching material, and this state of affairs is hardly surprising as producing original materials is a difficult and time-consuming process. Moreover, it would not make practical or economic sense for teachers to spend long hours duplicating one another's efforts by creating huge quantities of individually-produced material.

Published coursebooks are normally written by experienced and well-qualified people and the material contained in them is usually carefully tested in pilot studies in actual teaching situations before publication. Teachers can therefore be assured that coursebooks from reputable publishers will serve them well, if properly selected and used. I used the word *serve* advisedly because coursebooks are good servants but poor masters. The teacher should use the coursebook actively, by which I mean that the teacher should formulate objectives with the needs of the learners in mind and then seek out published material which will achieve those objectives. No teacher should permit the coursebook to set the objectives, let alone allow 'teaching the coursebook' to *be* the objective.

Teachers who express their teaching objectives in terms such as 'finishing unit 16', 'doing the first eight chapters' or 'reaching page 81' are acting as a servant of the coursebook rather than as its master (unless of course they are only using a convenient shorthand for well thought-out objectives). The teacher who makes active and positive use of his course materials on the other hand is the one who, firstly, has established and defined his objectives (probably in terms of what the students should be able to *do* in English, and then in terms of the structures, vocabulary, etc. necessary to equip them to do it) and, secondly, actively searches out teaching materials which will positively help in achieving these objectives. It is to this, second, kind of teacher that the contents of this book will I hope be useful.

There is a plethora of English language teaching material available on the market, covering many different aspects of language learning and language use. It ranges from comprehensive general courses, in several volumes and supported by visual and taped material, to specialised books which concentrate on one aspect of English, such as intonation, or one specific skill, such as writing. Other books deal with special kinds of English such as the language of medicine or engineering. Yet others offer exercises for certain stages in the learning process, such as practice exercises to give students greater ease in manipulating grammatical structures which have already been presented initially elsewhere.

Faced with this mass of teaching material, what should the teacher do when he has to make a choice and select a particular book or course from what is available? Does he choose the book with the nicest illustrations? Or does he choose the one that is the most comfortable to hold? Or should he perhaps go for the cheapest? Certainly these are not unimportant considerations, but there are many other factors involved that have at least equal claim on the teacher's attention. As in most decision making, the key lies in asking the right questions and evaluating the answers.

2 Good courses and bad courses

We may ask ourselves the obvious questions, 'Is course X a good course or a bad course? Is it better than course Y?' What makes a good course and what makes a bad course? It is certainly possible to identify courses which follow sound principles of language teaching and courses which are perhaps less soundly-based. The general principles which are outlined later in this chapter will provide us with some useful guidance here. But these questions can really only be answered by another question, 'Good for what and bad for whom?' In other words, we are not attempting to make absolute judgements in the abstract; we are concerned with making relative judgements, taking the learning situation into consideration. Even the more general kind of evaluation, where the teacher does not have a particular class or group of students in mind, will have as one of its aims to identify the type of learner for whom the coursebook would be suitable, taking into account age, nationality, native language, interests and objectives of the possible users. Size of class, availability of equipment and the amount of money available to spend on books will also be important factors.

English is taught in an enormously wide variety of situations throughout the world and a course suitable for adult learners in small groups in northern Europe is most unlikely to be suitable for a very large secondary school class in Africa. Some courses are quite specific about the kind of learner they cater for, and many coursebooks are written for learners of a particular age and native language who live in a specific cultural context. Courses produced according to the specifications of a national ministry of education for use in, say, secondary schools fall into this category and the writers will be familiar with the interests, backgrounds and abilities of the pupils who will use the material. An example of this is the *Nile Course for the Sudan* by M.R. Bates (Longman 1979). Because it draws on and relates to the life and culture of the Sudan, we may expect that it would be less useful elsewhere, and would not be suitable at all for use in countries which differ markedly from the Sudan.

Many courses however are general, not only in that they attempt to teach all aspects of English but also in that they are designed to satisfy a general worldwide market and are meant to be as usable in Chile as they would be in China. Such courses do not have one particular group of learners in mind and therefore usually take an English-speaking country as a setting along with corresponding sets of cultural values.

3 What the coursebooks say about themselves

As we have seen, different courses have different aims and claim to reach different objectives, so let us take a look at what some of the coursebooks say about themselves. We shall gain an impression of the potentially confusing variety of aims and methods that abound in the world of English language teaching materials.

Encounters aims to provide an interesting, useful and systematic introduction to the English language for complete beginners and for students who have learned a little English but need to make a fresh start.

(From *Encounters* by J. Garton-Sprenger *et al* (Heinemann Educational Books))

Kernel One is a course in English for complete or near beginners.
Kernel One has a careful structural progression with specific communicative aims.

(From *Kernel One* by R. O'Neill (Longman))

Starting Strategies is a new beginners' course for students aged 14 or over... It presents a totally new approach to language learning for students as it takes account of basic communication needs as its first priority.

(From *Starting Strategies* by B. Abbs and I. Freebairn (Longman))

This course is designed for... the learner who feels that learning English is difficult and that it has hitherto been irrelevant to his experience.
The main aim of the course is to provide the learner with the language he might need to take an active part in a wide range of social situations.

(From *Strategies* by B. Abbs, A. Ayton and I. Freebairn (Longman))

Kernel Lessons Plus is designed to:
1 provide material and exercise for, and promote the skills of listening, speaking, reading and writing;
2 provide a graded progression of structures and patterns at the pre-advanced level of learning;
3 provide material for the systematic revision of structures that should have been learned before;

(From *Kernel Lessons Plus* by R. O'Neill (Longman))

The purpose of this book is to give overseas students the opportunity to practise with current informational English. It also gives a very practical introduction to many basic aspects of modern British life.

(From *Practical Information* by B.J. Thomas (Edward Arnold))

> Our aim in writing this course has been to provide students who are learning composition-writing with detailed guidance in language and subject matter, but at the same time to leave them with the opportunity for personal expression.

(From *Guided Course in English Composition* by T.C. Jupp and J. Milne (Heinemann Educational Books))

> A large number of people are learning English not to study the language itself but to study other subjects through English. *Reading and Thinking in English* is based on the belief that a special kind of course is required for students of English whose main need is to gain access to information through English. The course has been designed for a wide range of learners whose needs can be described as 'English for Academic Purposes'.

(From *Reading and Thinking in English* (O.U.P))

> The aim of this new edition of *Advanced English Practice* remains the same as that of the original edition: to provide a variety of language material for foreign students at advanced level...The book provides ample material for consolidating the student's grasp of fundamentals and for revising those structures that students constantly have difficulty in mastering, before proceeding to a more mature examination of structure and vocabulary.

(From *Advanced English Practice* by B.D. Graver (O.U.P))

> ...units begin with a short statement of what is to be learnt; exercises ask for thought as well as language manipulation, and situations are mentally provoking and illustrative of varieties of English...Each unit covers a set of related grammar points well known for their difficulty for most learners.

(From *English in Mind* by C. Ttofi and T.S. Creed (Macmillan))

> INSIGHT
> Provides practice material suitable for any programme of intermediate language study where the aim is the improvement of both oral and written skills.

(From *Insight* by D. Byrne and S. Holden (Longman))

> This book teaches some of the intonation patterns used in conversation...It consists of ten units, each of them about particular aspects of the functions and interactions of conversation.

(From *Using Intonation* by V.J. Cook (Longman))

Three main perspectives on English language teaching can be identified from these extracts:

(a) *The communicative (or functional) perspective* which views language as above all a medium of communication between people.

(b) *The structural perspective* which sees language as a system of grammar and vocabulary.

(c) *The skills perspective* which emphasises the four skills of listening, speaking, reading and writing.

A further dimension is added when reference is made to the specialised needs of the learners, for instance those whose needs are English for academic purposes.

Coursebooks are in no way bound to adopt one approach to the exclusion of all others, and indeed many do try to achieve a working balance between them. However these perspectives are useful tools for the analysis of course materials, and I shall be developing them and exploiting them later in this book.

4 Some principles for materials evaluation

Despite the various approaches, of which we have seen some examples, and the even greater variety of learning/teaching situations in which students and teachers find themselves, there are certain general principles, based on good language-teaching practice, which will help us in our task of evaluating coursebooks. These principles underlie many of the more specific points which will be made in the subsequent chapters of this book.

4.1 Relate the teaching materials to your aims and objectives.

It is very important that the teaching materials used should take the learner forward as directly as possible towards his objectives. The objectives should be decided first, in line with the overall aim of the teaching programme, and then materials should be sought which can be related to these objectives. The aims of a teaching programme should determine the course materials to be used and not vice-versa.

4.2 Be aware of what language is for and select teaching materials which will help equip your students to use language effectively for their own purposes.

Our teaching must have at its base a consideration of what our students need to learn, that is, what they will do with English on completing their course. This involves the teacher in looking beyond the confines of the classroom into the outside world, and focusing his or her attention on the use that the individual learner will make of what he has learned, in a situation which is not primarily a learning situation. What we are looking at here is essentially the distinction between participation in a language drill, a coursebook dialogue or a role-play on the one hand, and on the other hand the ability to carry through a real transaction, the ability to express one's feelings or attitudes about real things or events to people who in no way form part of a formal learning situation. This distinction is not an entirely clear-cut one: for example, students taking part in a simulation in the classroom may indeed be effecting transactions and expressing attitudes which, within the artificial framework of the activity, are examples of genuine communication; equally, a foreign learner using English outside the classroom may occasionally be corrected by a well-intentioned listener. The essential difference however remains: in one case we have language used primarily in a learning situation and in the other we have language used primarily for communicative interaction.

There is without the slightest doubt a place in English language teaching for the drill and the coursebook dialogue and, indeed, that place will often be a large one. But we should always remember that such activities are a means to an end and never an end in themselves. The real aim of language teaching is to bring the learner to a point where he can use the language for his own purposes, and this goes far beyond manipulating structure drills.

4.3 Keep your students' learning needs in mind.

By **learning needs** I mean not so much the actual language to be learned as the way in which it is selected, graded, presented and practised. In order to learn effectively and efficiently, students should meet only small pieces of new language at one time, what we might call **learning units**. These learning units should be related to each other in such a way that the learner can relate new language to what he already knows and can build up his knowledge of English by adding new learning units to his existing body of knowledge.

But learning needs are not limited solely to considerations of the language. Learners have intellectual and emotional needs too. Learning a language is difficult and demanding (teachers can easily overlook this!) and students need to be encouraged and stimulated as they progress. This is largely the teacher's job, but course materials can help by using subject matter that is intellectually stimulating and to which the students can relate personally. It is also important that materials should be usable with whole classes of learners, with small groups, and with individuals. This is because students need to be catered for both as individuals and as members of a group. Within the space of one lesson, a student may act alternately as an individual and a group member, depending on several factors including the sort of exercise he is doing, the skills that are being practised and his own learning strategies.

4.4 Consider the relationship between language, the learning process and the learner.

All three are vital aspects of language teaching and it is essential that teaching materials should keep all three constantly in view and never become so preoccupied with one that the others are lost sight of. It must be said that much traditional teaching material put out in the 1960s places considerable emphasis on language and on the desired linguistic performance of the learner, but tends to neglect the learner as an individual by imposing rigid teaching methods and presupposing equally rigid learning processes. What we do know about language-learning processes leads us to believe that there is no one 'best' way of learning and that learners adopt different learning strategies, often switching strategies from time to time.

Certain more recent approaches to language learning tend to concentrate very heavily on the individual, on the individual's desires and feelings, but neglect rather to come to grips with some of the linguistic difficulties inherent in language learning. Learning activities, no matter how interesting and involving, will not be of much help to the learner of English unless they present and practise English in a systematic and comprehensive way so that new language items can be assimilated by the learner. There is currently something of a tendency to use activities for their own sake, because they are enjoyable or because they 'work' as activities, without due regard to their value as language-learning exercises. Of course the things our students do in class should be interesting and enjoyable, but they should also be carefully examined in terms of their language-teaching potential.

5 The principles in practice
A case study of *Encounters*

In order to illustrate what we might expect to find in a well-designed general course, and at the same time to look at the principles in practice, I will examine some characteristics of *Encounters* (Garton-Sprenger *et al*, 1979), a course for beginners comprising ten units each of seven lessons plus a Language Study section, and see how the application of our general principles for evaluation throws into focus significant features of the course. Coursebooks vary considerably and the features of *Encounters* which will be identified are not the only ones which would be acceptable: they are included here for the purpose of giving practical examples. Other courses can be shown to meet our expectations in other, equally appropriate, ways.

The overall aims and objectives of *Encounters* are clearly stated in the introduction to the Teachers' Book. The course is intended for complete beginners or false beginners (those who have learned a little English but need a fresh start). It is a general course suitable for learners from about age fifteen onwards (although this is not stated in the Teachers' Book) and provides work for about 180 hours of study. The potential application of this coursebook is therefore very wide. It is intended for use in a world context and was not designed with one particular country in mind. The cultural background is British, but not strongly so, and the book has an international flavour but is oriented towards the western world.

The learning objectives are expressed primarily in terms of communicative functions within the range of three main themes:
Talking about yourself as an individual
Talking about physical surroundings
Interaction between the individual and the environment
These themes have been selected on the basis of their usefulness to the learner, their intrinsic interest and the amount of complexity and unpredictability that an elementary learner can cope with.

The communicative functions, such as greetings, requests, apologies and suggestions, derive from the main themes, and had been selected before the language forms (structures, vocabulary, etc.) were decided on. The writers put it this way in the Teachers' Book:

> We consider that the language functions . . . should be chosen *first*, and the linguistic content, the structures, should be finalised at the *second stage*. In this way the learner practises and is made aware of the way English is used from the outset of the course as well as building up a systematic understanding and mastery of language forms.

The language forms which realise these functions:

> have been selected on the basis of their range of use and of lin-
> guistic simplicity and structural grading. (. . .) The process of
> syllabus design has been one of continually choosing and
> modifying both forms and functions so that they fit together and
> represent as useful and as simple a progression for the learner as
> possible. (. . .) The final language syllabus consists of one sylla-
> bus of functions and one of structures, and the structural sylla-
> bus serves the purposes of the functional one.

The objectives of the course, then, are to take the beginner and equip him to use English in a limited range of situations, determined by the three main themes. The language he learns will be useful and have communicative potential, but it will also be structurally relatively simple and will be graded as the course progresses according to increasing complexity. The basis on which the course is designed combines usefulness and application in the outside world with 'learnability' in the classroom, and therefore seems to be realistic and practicable. It is interesting to note how the writers have implicitly concluded that, at an elementary level at least, a functional syllabus without reference to structures would be as unworkable in the classroom as a structural syllabus without reference to its communicative potential would be unusable in the outside world.

Given that few teachers would disagree with the underlying assumption that language is learned in order to be used, it is up to the individual teacher to decide whether the aims of the coursebook match up with his own teaching aims. Our **first principle** (4.1) requires the coursebook to match the students' learning objectives, so we must now ask ourselves: does the coursebook teach the sort of communicative abilities, in the sort of situations, that we want? Is what the coursebook writers consider interesting actually going to be comprehensible and acceptable to our students? If learning to express functions such as introducing yourself, describing places, asking for and giving directions, expressing likes and dislikes, apologizing and making suggestions is relevant to our students' needs and interests, then *Encounters* may well, in terms of its objectives, be suitable. Such functions are so universal that it is hard to imagine many learners who will not need to use them at some stage in their lives, but the actual situations in which the functions are expressed will differ according to cultural background. In evaluating the material we need to decide whether the settings used in the coursebook are sufficiently close to those in which the students will find themselves to be meaningful and acceptable.

We should always bear in mind however that, as the writers of *Encounters* point out:

> textbooks are only an aid to the language-learning process,
> which also depends upon individuals, their needs and their
> relationships in the classroom. Teachers and students find their
> own ways of using a textbook to suit these circumstances, and to
> suit their own methods of learning.

No coursebook will be totally suited to a particular teaching situation. The teacher will have to find his own way of using it and adapting it if necessary. So we should not be looking for the perfect coursebook which meets all our requirements, but rather for the best possible fit between what the coursebook offers and what we as teachers and students need.

Encounters, as we have already seen, puts considerable emphasis on *using* English, and therefore should satisfy the demands of our **second principle** to select materials which will help equip students to use language effectively for their own purposes. At the presentation stage, the writers state that:

> the aim . . . of each lesson is to show the learner how the new language is *used.*

This is done by presenting new language items in a clear context:

> the aim is the demonstration of the target language functions in an authentic context

and on completion of the presentation section the students should understand how English is used to convey a particular function, as well as understanding the new structures and vocabulary presented. In other words, structures and vocabulary are learned in context so that the student learns not only what they are but also how to use them. At the practice stage a wide variety of activities are used to give the students adequate practice in using what they have learned in realistic situations.

Let us take one lesson of *Encounters* (Lesson 22) and see how this works out in practice. The lesson is reproduced on pages 10 and 11. The communicative aim is two-fold:

Enquiring about and stating likes and dislikes
Expressing disagreement
and the new structures used to realise these functions are:
Questions introduced by auxiliary DO   Do you like . . . ?
Questions introduced by WHO   Who's . . . ?
Short answers   Yes, I do/No, I don't
Statements of agreement and disagreement   So do I/I don't

The initial presentation is through a dialogue, put in context by the introductory paragraph which the teacher reads and discusses with the class, ensuring that the relationship between the speakers is fully understood. The dialogue does not contain many examples of new structures, the reason given being that it must appear realistic, and that in real language use we meet a variety of structures rather than the same one or two repeated several times. (Compare this with a mechanical language drill!) What the dialogue does achieve is to exemplify in a natural way the functions which are being taught.

Each function and new structure is then practised in controlled exercises cued by visuals. These controlled exercises however are not just mechanical drills because they allow the student, within the linguistic framework of the vocabulary and structures available to him, to express his own likes and dislikes and to agree and disagree as he wishes.

The Survey activity adds a further dimension by setting up a situation where students gather information from each other and about each other, necessarily asking and answering questions, and then record the answers in writing. These activities, within the context of the classroom, are genuinely communicative and give students the opportunity to use English to a purposeful end even at a stage when their range of structures and vocabulary is severely limited.

LESSON 22

**Talking about likes and dislikes (1)
Books and films**

Sam Miller is a student at art college in
London. Jill Archer is also a student. Jill is at
London University and she is studying
Spanish. Sam and Jill do not know each other
very well. One day they meet in a bookshop.

SAM: Hello, Jill.
JILL.: Hi, Sam. How are you?
SAM: Fine. What are you looking at?
JILL.: *Small is Beautiful.* It's a book about
        modern society.
SAM: How boring!
JILL.: No, it isn't. It's very interesting. What
        kind of books do you like?
SAM: Detective stories.
JILL.: So do I.

PRACTICE

   Study

Kinds of books

Detective stories

Art books

WOMEN TODAY

Books about society

Books about …

Romantic novels

Kinds of films

Westerns   Comedies

Documentaries

Horror films

…films

   Ask each other

Examples:
Do you like detective stories?
Yes, I do./No, I don't.
Do you like horror films?
Yes, I do./No, I don't.

   Tell each other

Examples:
I like detective stories.
So do I./I don't.
I like westerns.
So do I./I don't.

56

Survey

Unit 4

Write out a questionnaire and complete for other students.

Example:
1. Who's your favourite author?
   Agatha Christie.

QUESTIONNAIRE				
	Student A	Student B	Student C	Student D
1. Favourite Author	Agatha Christie			
2. Favourite Singer	Denis Roussos			
3. Favourite Film Star	Humphrey Bogart			
4. Favourite Sport	Tennis			
5. Favourite Colour	Blue			

English for the classroom – Pronunciation

Ask your teacher about six difficult words in Unit 4.

Example:
How do you pronounce C-H-R-I-S-T-I-E, please?

Write sentences

Write three sentences about books or films you like.
Write three sentences about books or films you don't like.

Example:
I like detective stories. They are very exciting. My favourite
author is Agatha Christie.

Language Study Exercises 4.1 4.3

57

Fig. 1. (From *Encounters* by J. Garton-Sprenger *et al* (Heinemann Educational Books))

Another characteristic of real language use is that the user normally has a greater receptive ability than productive ability. That is to say, he can understand things that he would not be able to express easily. For instance, I might be able to understand a car repair manual, but I would find it difficult to write one because I would lack the productive ability to use the correct terminology. The writers of *Encounters* suggest that:

> . . . if the development of all four skills is tied to the rate of learning of productive spoken language, much of what is required for the other three skills will not be learned.

Their aim is for understanding to develop faster than speaking and for reading to develop faster than writing, so that the learner's performance in the different skills to some extent reflects that of the native speaker. So, the learner is not expected to be able to say everything that he hears or reads, nor is he expected to be able to write everything that he hears or reads. This allows the learner to develop his reading strategies, for example, to a point where at the end of the book he can read and understand a simple letter or questionnaire, even though he might not be able to write either.

So far as equipping our students to use English effectively is concerned we may fairly conclude that *Encounters* goes a very long way in meeting the need and makes great efforts to provide meaningful presentation and practice.

Our **third principle** (4.3) was to keep our students' learning needs in mind. So far as selection, grading, presentation and practice are concerned, we have already made our evaluation, so let us now consider the extent to which the intellectual and personal needs of our learners are met. That is, whether the coursebook interests and involves the student. The writers claim to adopt a **learner-centred approach** which encourages the teacher to make use of the knowledge and interests of the students so that the classroom activities become 'relevant and spontaneous'.

The Survey activity from Lesson 22 already referred to meets these criteria and so do these projects and discussion activities, taken from lessons 61 and 62 respectively:

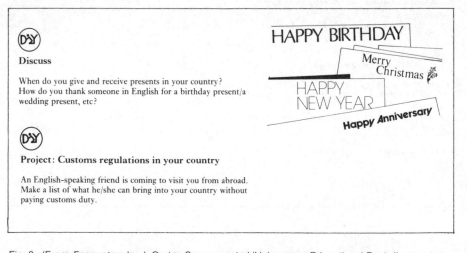

Discuss

When do you give and receive presents in your country?
How do you thank someone in English for a birthday present/a wedding present, etc?

Project: Customs regulations in your country

An English-speaking friend is coming to visit you from abroad. Make a list of what he/she can bring into your country without paying customs duty.

Fig. 2. (From *Encounters* by J. Garton-Sprenger *et al* (Heinemann Educational Books))

One of the most difficult aspects of writing materials at elementary level is providing exercises and activities which are structurally simple enough for beginners and yet intellectually stimulating enough for intelligent adults or children. The writers of *Encounters* have gone some way towards solving this difficulty, but it remains a problem, and some of the activities which are intended to engage the interest of the learners may seem rather thin and insubstantial to the more sophisticated among them. One partial solution is to treat the activities as something of a game rather than as something very serious. Fortunately this problem becomes much less difficult to cope with at intermediate and advanced levels.

Our **fourth principle** (4.4) concerns the learner and the language, and the learning process which, as it were, brings the two together. We are looking here for a balance between the needs of the learner on the one hand, and, on the other hand, the constraints imposed by the necessity of learning the structures and vocabulary of English. It is all very well talking, as we have done, about learning useful functions of English, but it must always be remembered that these functions cannot be expressed without a good working knowledge of the grammar and vocabulary, not to mention the sound system, of English.

How does *Encounters* achieve a balance between the learner's communicative needs, the learning process and the structure of the English language? We have already seen how the syllabus of the course was determined in the first instance by functional considerations, and how the structural syllabus was derived from the functional syllabus and serves the purposes of the functional syllabus. The learners' communicative needs are quite well catered for by the functional syllabus, and indeed a glimpse at the contents page will show that the primary organisation of the course is in terms of communicative function. The structural grading within the functional framework is equally clear, and the Teachers' Book provides a structural reference list which identifies each structure taught and gives the unit in which it was introduced.

Additionally, at the end of each unit there is a Language Study component which revises and summarises the structures presented in that unit. This provides the student with practice in the manipulation of language form, which is necessary for the development of oral fluency, and with a convenient checklist of structures that he has learned. This very valuable reinforcement of language forms already presented and practised in a functional context helps to establish a balance of emphasis between **language function** and **language form** (see p. 15 for a more detailed discussion of this relationship).

So far as the learning process is concerned, the coursebook writers acknowledge that people learn in different ways and that learning is an individual process. Their strategy for coping with this is to provide as much variety as possible and to avoid dogmatically adopting one particular view of language learning or one particular methodology. This approach is intended to allow the teacher to select material that best suits his own students' approach to learning. Unfortunately, for practical reasons, no coursebook can offer a large number of alternative ways of teaching each item on the syllabus, and even when adopting an eclectic approach, coursebook writers must of necessity make their own value judgements and opt for one kind of presentation rather than another. As I have suggested earlier, it is really up to the individual teacher to be sensitive to his students' learning strategies and to adapt and supplement the main coursebook where necessary.

Our brief look at *Encounters* has highlighted many very positive features which make it an attractive coursebook for teenage and adult beginners (particularly from the western world) who are embarking on a general course and hope to be able to use the English that they learn at an early stage. No coursebook is wholly complete and *Encounters* is no exception. For instance, it only touches briefly on the **intonation** of English and supplementary materials would probably be needed in this area. But as no coursebook will be ideally suited to your particular style of teaching, it will almost always be necessary to supplement the material and adapt it. Some ideas on doing this will be found in Chapter 9 of this book.

Conclusion

The advice offered in this book is based on these premises:

(a) The learner is an individual who also functions as part of a group. He has individual needs and collective needs. These needs are both intellectual and affective.
(b) English, like other languages, is a complex system of language forms which convey meaning and allow the speaker to perform communicative acts. Language behaviour is part of, and intimately bound in with, social behaviour and cannot be fully understood except in the social context.
(c) The teacher's role is to promote learning through the use of his professional skills and knowledge of the students' learning processes. The teacher also needs to understand the structure of English and how it is used for communication between individuals.
(d) The role of the coursebook is to aid the learner and the teacher in accomplishing this task.

Exercises and activities

(a) Look at the introduction to a coursebook which you use or which you know, referring to Teacher's Book if possible, and list the objectives which are stated in it.

(b) How far do you think that the objectives which you identified in activity (a) are appropriate to the learning needs of the students or pupils for whom the coursebook was designed?

(c) Note down three or four of the most important things that you would like to see in a general course. Discuss them if possible with your colleagues or with other members of your group, build up a composite list and try to put the items roughly in order of importance.

2 The Language Content

In this chapter we are looking at *what* is being taught in terms of grammar and vocabulary and also in terms of meaning, function and appropriateness. Nor must we neglect to consider the different language skills being taught. It is clear that different students have differing needs so far as what they learn is concerned, so this chapter is largely descriptive and aims to establish the nature of the language contained in the course material. Evaluation of its suitability for particular types of learner is left until later when the content of the course material is matched with potential users of the material. This is dealt with particularly in Chapters 7 and 8.

1 Form and Function

What aspects of the language system are taught? To what extent is the material based upon or organised around the teaching of **language form, language function,** and **patterns of communicative interaction?**

Suppose we wish to teach a particular function, such as 'expressing that others are not obliged to do something'. The term **function** really refers to the process of conveying the meaning that 'somebody is not obliged to do something'. It is clear that this meaning is ordinarily conveyed through language form (words and sounds organised according to the rules of the language) although it could in certain circumstances be conveyed by non-verbal means such as, in this case, a shrug of the shoulders or a shake of the head. The language forms available to us in English to express this particular function are quite numerous and include:

You don't have to...
You needn't...
It's not obligatory for you to...
It's not compulsory for you to...
There's no obligation to...
It's up to you.
You're free to choose.
It's completely voluntary.

Therefore we have to make a selection from the possible forms which can be used to express a function. Coursebooks must teach language form because meaning and function are expressed through form and without form there could be no verbal communication. The crucial question is whether language is presented solely or predominantly as form – in which case the material will concentrate on helping the learner to produce grammatically correct sentences without too much concern for how these sentences would be used – or whether the function of language items is also taught. Put another way, is language presented as a closed grammatical system or is it presented as a communicative system in a context of use and so as an integral part of the pattern of social behaviour?

It is orthodox now in writing on language teaching to contrast the structural approach to course design and the functional approach in terms of how the content is selected and organised: in units of language form in the first case and in functional units in the second. No one, however, can produce a functional course without also teaching language form, so we are not really choosing to teach *either* structures *or* functions: we should teach both. What needs to be looked at is not so much whether the material is wholly structural or wholly functional, but how the relationships, often very complex ones, between form and function are handled and put over to the learner. Whether we label 'could you shut the door' as an example of a modal verb plus a lexical verb with a complement, or as an example of the function of making a polite request, is less important than how successfully we teach the relationship between the form of the sentence and its effective use in a context of social interaction.

A further consideration is whether patterns of communicative interaction are taught. When we use language, we do not use sentences in isolation from each other. In any piece of natural language, whether it is a conversation or a written text, sentences relate to each other in their meanings and their functions; they do not simply occur as isolated bits of language. There are rules and conventions for the linking of sentences to form larger units of discourse, and we should expect to find built into a course models and examples of sentence linking (not sentence joining, but linking sentences which remain structurally separate). For example, in a coursebook for writing-skills we should expect guidance on not only how to write sentences that are grammatical but also on writing paragraphs, including when to start a new paragraph, and on writing longer passages of English composed of several paragraphs.

The following extract is an exercise in reading and, specifically, in recognising some of the links that are to be found between sentences in a passage of written English.

---

7 Reference: connectives

In writing, and especially when writing explanations, we often have to refer back to an earlier word or idea. To make it clear that it is something we have mentioned before, we often use *this* or *these*, or sometimes *the*. In addition, to avoid repeating exactly the same word again and again, we use another word – either a different part of speech (e.g. if we use a verb the first time, we may change it to a noun the second time), or a word that has a similar meaning, or a more general word.

For example:

First Reference	Later Reference
The water evaporates.	This evaporation
It moves	This movement
It enlarges	This enlargement
There are changes	These variations
The temperature falls	This drop in temperature
The wood is cut with an axe.	This method of cutting
The numbers can be added, multiplied etc.	These mathematical operations
The product can be advertised on radio, TV etc.	These means of advertising

8 Petroleum

Read the following passage on petroleum.

In the shallow waters off the coast a few hundred million years ago, vast numbers of minute creatures and plants lived and died. Owing to the lack of oxygen, the remains of *these marine organisms* were unable to decompose. As a result of climatic changes, *these coastal areas* became buried under layers of earth, and *the organic remains* were subjected to high pressures and temperatures over periods of millions of years. *These conditions* caused the decomposition and the chemical breakdown of the fats, carbohydrates and proteins in the remains. As the conditions of decomposition varied from one region to another, petroleum found in different parts of the world varies considerably in composition. In the course of time petroleum was squeezed out of the original source rock into more porous rocks, in *some of which* it accumulated.

To what earlier words or phrases do the phrases in italics refer?

Fig. 3. (From *Think and Link* by J. Cooper (Edward Arnold))

Language learning, then, may be seen as acquisition of the ability to participate in the dynamic and creative process of communication, and not just an acquisition of separate, isolated units of language, whether they are termed structural units or functional units. We should ask ourselves to what extent the teaching material reflects this view.

2 Aspects of language form

Which aspects of language form are taught: **phonology** (the production of individual sounds, stress, rhythm and intonation), **grammar** (morphology and syntax), **vocabulary** (lexis), **discourse** (sequence of sentences)?

One might expect that any course material which aimed to teach the spoken language would teach the phonology or sound system of English in the same ordered and systematic way that we are accustomed to finding in the teaching of grammatical structures. However this is not always the case, even in comprehensive general courses, and phonology is often at best taught incidentally and in random order. There seems theoretically to be little justification for this state of affairs: we would not expose our students to grammar in a random and unsystematic way and simply expect them to perceive the underlying patterns and rules. Why then do coursebooks follow this procedure with the teaching of the sound system of English?

The answer probably lies in the immense difficulty of producing a course that is well graded at several levels of language simultaneously. To grade the introduction of grammatical items and vocabulary, to present them in context and to give exponents of them that show coherent functional organisation so that the grammar, etc. is seen to meet the learner's communicative needs, is a difficult enough task for the coursebook writer to face up to and he often finds that incorporating a systematic and carefully graded phonology-teaching component simultaneously is well-nigh impossible. Considering, for example, the complexity of intonation, it seems hardly surprising that intonation patterns occur more or less randomly in even elementary coursebooks.

The practical answer for the teacher is to use specialised material produced for pronunciation teaching in parallel with the main coursebook, so that the learners do get a systematic familiarisation with the elements of phonology. For our purposes this example identifies one of the positive benefits of materials evaluation and analysis: it spotlights both the strengths and weaknesses of coursebooks and identifies for the teacher areas of language teaching which require the use of supplementary materials.

Most coursebooks concentrate heavily on the teaching of grammatical structures and on the whole do it well. Grammar is immensely important, being the system of rules for the formation of correct sentences and it is essential that learners are able to both understand and use the rules of grammar. Few, if any, writers on language learning would disagree that the internalisation of grammar rules is central to language learning and that any teaching programme which omits grammar is not really teaching language in the full sense of the word. In order to create language which expresses what he wants to say, the learner must be able to use the rules of grammar.

The introduction of vocabulary in coursebooks tends to be variable. In some cases vocabulary items are seen as isolated units to be slotted into grammatical structures and bearing no relationship to other vocabulary items. Other courses do their best to teach vocabulary as part of a structural system by identifying and exploiting relationships between words. The latter approach would appear to be the better, as learning theory and empirical evidence suggest that items are learned and recalled more readily if relationships can be perceived between the items forming the system (see Stevick 1976, chapter 2). The lexicon of English is structured in various ways, both formally and semantically, and it is therefore desirable that this structuring should be exploited for learning purposes (see Richards 1976).

I have used the word **discourse** on page 16 as one of the aspects of language form to look for in a coursebook. (See 2.2 in the checklist in Chapter 10.) This refers to the way in which sentences are linked (but not joined) in order to produce a complete unit of language which forms a self-contained whole. This whole may be a newspaper article, a letter, an advertisement or even a public notice. What we are particularly concerned about here is whether or not the coursebook teaches the student to understand and produce whole units of language and if it indicates any of the rules and conventions for doing so. Many courses do this implicitly or partially, for example they may teach how to write a paragraph or how to begin a conversation with a greeting, but few explicitly set themselves the task of dealing comprehensively with this level of organisation of language.

3 Appropriateness

What explicit reference is there to **appropriateness** (the matching of language to its social context and function)? How systematically is it taught? How fully and comprehensively is it taught? This concept is familiar to most EFL teachers. **Appropriateness** or, as it is sometimes called, appropriacy, means in this context stylistic appropriateness. The concept really derives from work done on communicative competence and from the now classic statement by Hymes (1971, p. 278), 'There are rules of use without which the rules of grammar would be useless.' When we use language, we need to be able to perceive the social situation in which we are operating and to be able to match the language we use to the situation.

For the foreign learner, as for the young child acquiring his native language, there is a double task: to perceive the social situations and to select appropriate language. One aspect of the task is non-linguistic and the other is linguistic, but they are so closely connected that the language teacher cannot afford to neglect either aspect. Cultural gaps pose problems to learners of English, particularly where the social, political or religious differences are great. I recall from my own experience a case where a Chinese speaker of English was looking after an American professor on a lecture tour of China. After the American's first lecture the Chinese, using a standard formula of politeness in China, told the lecturer that he looked tired and asked him to take a rest. The American interpreted this as a criticism of his performance and was somewhat displeased. When something of this nature happens, effective communication has not taken place.

We may therefore justifiably ask the extent to which a language-teaching coursebook teaches these important rules of use, how competently it does it, and how systematically.

4 Varieties

What kind of English is taught: **dialect** (class, geographic), **style** (formal, neutral, informal), **occupational register, medium** (written, spoken)?

Much has been written on varieties of English and I will limit myself to identifying some salient points which are of importance to the language teacher. There are many dialects of English, both geographical dialects and class dialects, but the kind of English presented in coursebooks is usually either standard, middle-class, educated, southern British English or standard, middle-class, educated, American English. Other dialects of English do not figure prominently except in materials produced for a very localised market. Whilst there seem to be very good reasons for teaching one of the two dialects mentioned above (perhaps the strongest reason being that they have the widest intelligibility in the English-speaking world), there may be special situations where a *receptive* knowledge of a less widely used dialect is needed. Examples which spring to mind are students going to study in Glasgow, and businessmen going to make deals in Jamaica or Nigeria.

Stylistic variation, and in particular the difference between formal, neutral and informal language, is important in that it is necessary for stylistic appropriateness. This has been dealt with briefly above.

We may also ask ourselves if the material that we are evaluating has any instances of specific occupational register, i.e. a style of English characteristically associated, through, for example, its specialised vocabulary, with a particular occupation. We are likely to find this frequently with ESP material, but rarely elsewhere.

Differences between speech and writing are fundamental and far reaching and need to be taken into account in materials evaluation. Are the examples of English given characteristic of speech or writing, or does the material contain both? We may also ask to what extent dialogues which purport to be speech are in fact characteristic of authentic speech. It is probably mistaken to suggest that models of speech for EFL teaching should always be examples of authentic English, but they certainly should incorporate some of the features of authentic spoken English and should not be 'spoken written English', i.e. English which exhibits the characteristics of written English but is spoken. For a discussion of the relationship between speech and writing see Byrne (1979, chapters 1 and 2) or Stubbs (1980, chapter 2).

5 Language skills

What language skills are taught: **receptive** (written/reading, spoken/listening), **productive** written/writing, spoken/speaking, **integration of skills** (e.g. note taking, dictation, reading aloud, participating in conversation), **translation** (into English/from English)?

We may reasonably ask what language skills the material teaches, using the conventional breakdown into receptive and productive skills, speech and writing. This gives us:

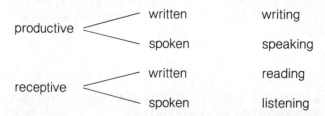

	written	writing
productive	spoken	speaking
receptive	written	reading
	spoken	listening

As we have seen earlier, it is necessary for teaching purposes to divide what is to be learned into small, assimilable units which the learner can absorb progressively. It is for this reason that we often talk about the 'four skills' as separate entities which are sometimes taught separately, one lesson emphasising listening, for example, and another writing. However, most communicative interactions through language involve the use of more than one 'skill': consider normal conversation for instance which involves both speaking and listening in rapid sequence, or taking a telephone message requiring both the above skills together with writing. We should therefore ask not only what emphasis the material places on each of the four skills but also the extent to which it provides practice in integrating the skills in models of real communication.

Summary

What we are looking for in a general course is material which presents different aspects of language as systematically as possible, having regard to the need to present new language items to the learner in small assimilable units, each unit related to what has gone before. The course should be as comprehensive as possible, including the teaching of pronunciation as well as the teaching of grammar and vocabulary. Some attention should also be given to linking sentences to form discourse and the learner should be prepared for real-life language use, such as taking part in conversations and other interactions. It is better for a coursebook to be too comprehensive than too insubstantial. A teacher can always omit to use material that is there. It is much more difficult to make good what the coursebook has left out.

Exercises and activities

(a) What is the balance in your coursebook between teaching the forms of English and the functions of English? Do you consider that more emphasis should be placed on form or function in your teaching situation? How does the coursebook establish links between form and function? (See question 2.1 in Chapter 10.)

(b) Consider the extent to which your coursebook provides material for pronunciation (see question 2.2 in Chapter 10). Do you consider that pronunciation is adequately dealt with? If not, what would you like to see?

(c) What variety of English is taught by your coursebook? Can you place it geographically and socially? (See question 2.4 In Chapter 10)

(d) How far does your coursebook prepare the learner for real communication in English? (See question 2.5 in Chapter 10.)

3 The Selection and Grading of Language Items

1 Functional syllabuses and structural syllabuses

Does the material follow a **structural syllabus** or a **functional syllabus**? A syllabus is an ordered statement of *what* is to be taught, but not a statement of how it is to be taught. It is ordered because it does not simply list language items to be taught, it also puts them in a sequence for teaching purposes. The coursebook writer must order his material according to some system, and in general he will devise his own progression. The content of a coursebook, what it teaches and in what order, may well act as a syllabus for many of the teachers who use the book.

The relationship between function and form has been referred to already in Chapter 2 and here I want to relate both function and form to the syllabus. In a **functional syllabus** the functions are selected and sequenced according to their usefulness to the learner, the extent to which they meet the learner's communicative needs. So the earliest items in the syllabus will be those that the learner will need most in the situations in which he will use English. How the syllabus designer predicts what these situations will be is very much a matter of subjective judgement. Whether he makes intelligent guesses or does some research, the results he comes up with will depend largely on his personal decisions.

Some advantages of the functional syllabus are that the learning goals can be identified in terms which make sense to the learners themselves. To the average student, 'making requests for information' means more than 'interrogative form of modal verbs followed by infinitive'. Also, by using the criterion of usefulness rather than grammatical factors, the syllabus designer ensures that the learning process has an immediate practical result in that the students can use what they have learned outside the classroom at a relatively early stage. Students who do not complete a course will still take away with them something useful in the form of a limited communicative ability in English.

The **structural syllabus** reflects a more traditional approach, and, taking as its starting point the internal structure of the language rather than its use, may be called subject-centred. The structural syllabus sequences the items of language to be taught in order of presumed difficulty, largely on the basis of complexity of structure. Structural syllabuses in traditional coursebooks show a striking uniformity in the sequencing of the items that they teach. This seems to depend on tradition and the accumulated practical wisdom of teachers, rather than on any scientific definition of which structures are more complex and more difficult to learn.

One limitation of the structural syllabus is the scant regard paid to meaning and especially to the communicative potential of what is taught. The essential objective of the structural syllabus seems to be the skill of manipulating language forms, with little concern for the functional meaning that the forms can be used to express.

The strength of the structural syllabus is that it can account for all the forms of language and relate them to each other in a coherent and finite system. The functional syllabus on the other hand lists various functions and gives examples of how those functions can be expressed in English.

Functions do not form an interrelated finite system, nor have they been fully described and delimited. Most lists of functions so far provided have been based upon introspection and intuition. Language forms are, after all, observable, whereas functions have to be inferred from their linguistic form and as such are more difficult to handle in a full, explicit and objective description.

Where a structural syllabus is adopted by a coursebook, we should check that sufficient attention has been paid to the meaning of the structures taught. One structure may have two or more meanings and it may be used differently according to the meaning which it expresses. The article (*the/a*) is a good example of this. With specific reference, definite and indefinite articles have a different meaning and play a different role in English syntax. So:

a book was lost yesterday

means something different from:

the book was lost yesterday.

The use of the definite article *the* in the second example indicates that the book is known to the speaker and listener and it is identifiable, whereas in the first example it is not. However, with general reference, the definite and indefinite articles, *the* and *a*, are virtually interchangeable. Compare:

the lion is a fine animal

with:

a lion is a fine animal.

There may be a fine shade of meaning which differentiates the two, but practically speaking either article can be used without a major change of meaning.

It is important that a coursebook should specify not only the structure that is being taught but also the particular meaning of that structure. Most coursebooks do make this distinction with major items of structure, such as the present continuous form of the verb, indicating for instance whether it is being taught with its future meaning or its present meaning. But in other areas of grammar, such as the article, many coursebooks are less careful.

Widdowson (1979 p. 248) points out that a functional syllabus is still only an inventory of units, functional rather than structural, and that there is no demonstration of the crucial relationship between form and function. The functional syllabus does not account for communicative competence because it does not contain the strategies for using linguistic elements for communicative purposes. Such strategies amount to more than just combining functional units learned in isolation and include 'an ability to *make* (create) sense as a participant in discourse... by the skilful deployment of shared knowledge of... language resources and rules of language use'.

Structural and functional syllabuses do not seem to be opposed to each other, as they have sometimes come to be seen, but are better considered as complementary. The functional perspective of a functional syllabus develops the structural syllabus by incorporating into it a component which is sensitive to the learner's communicative needs and provides him with units of communication as well as with units of linguistic forms.

2 Subject-centred approach and student-centred approach

Is the selection and sequence of the language to be taught based on an attempt to identify probable student need (**student-centred approach**) or the internal structure of the language (**subject-centred approach**)?

Here we are concerned in a general manner with the extent to which student need is taken into account, and more specifically with the suitability of the material being evaluated to the needs of a particular group of students.

Most course material is designed with a fairly general readership in mind. This applies particularly to general courses which aim to give learners a basic competence in most aspects of English at elementary and intermediate levels but it also applies, perhaps surprisingly, in ESP materials. Here one might expect a title such as 'English in Engineering' or 'English in Agriculture' to be very specific and to meet fairly exactly the needs of all engaged in those particular occupations. Clearly such courses are aimed at a much more narrowly defined market than are general courses, but nevertheless the specific needs of students using these materials will vary considerably, and the materials will display, within their field, a considerable degree of generalisation. Good examples of the degree of generalisation possible in ESP materials include courses which teach basic scientific concepts in English and courses which deal with various kinds of academic study skills, where the skills taught and practised include note-taking from lectures and from written texts, reading for information, and writing academic papers. Here we are really concerned with the student's ability to use English to perform certain tasks. The skills or abilities learned can then be applied in any of a wide range of situations.

When considering how far a piece of material meets the needs of a particular student or group of students, it is just as important to ask oneself what the material teaches the student to *do* in English as to ask oneself what sort of English is being taught.

Perhaps the kind of material most directly aimed at a specific sort of student is course material for examinations. Here the students, although they may be disparate in background and past history, share a common and clearly defined, if rather artificial, goal: to pass a particular examination. It is interesting to observe how examinations influence teaching and course content. This is the so-called **backwash effect** of examinations: passing the examination becomes the over-riding objective of the course, whether or not that really involves learning English as an authentic communicative system. The backwash effect puts a very heavy responsibility on examiners to ensure that what their examinations require candidates to do is truly and fully representative of genuine language use. The point is that where a formal examination is the goal, both teachers and coursebooks will prepare students for the examination whether or not what is examined is representative of language as a communicative process.

3 Grading and recycling

Is the **grading** of the language content steep, average or shallow? Is the **progression** linear or cyclical? Is there **adequate recycling** of grammar and vocabulary?

By **grading** we mean the speed with which the student progresses, how much new material is introduced in a given number of hours, how close together or how far apart new grammatical structures are in relation to each other, how much new vocabulary is introduced in each unit and so on. What is very important here is the amount of practice material provided, in the form of exercises and other activities such as open dialogues and role-plays, *after* one new language item has been presented and *before* the next one is introduced.

If, for example, the present continuous is introduced in unit 4 of a course, the *shall/will* future in unit 5, the simple past in unit 6 and the present perfect in unit 7 and each new grammar item has four or five practice exercises attached to it, then the course would be considered to be steeply graded. (I am taking a unit to be equivalent to about six hours' work in class.) Such a course would most probably not be intended for students learning these items for the first time but rather for false beginners, those who have previously learned English, perhaps at school, but, having either forgotten what they learned or failed to learn effectively the first time, are re-learning the language and, with the advantage of some previous if imperfect knowledge of English, can make faster progress than true beginners.

To take another example, a course which devoted six units to the present tense of the verb *to be* and then a further seven or eight units to the present continuous tense of lexical verbs would be considered to have a very shallow grading because each new item is very thoroughly presented and then practised in a variety of contexts before the next item is introduced. Such a course would be suitable for beginners who had had no previous contact with English and were experiencing difficulty in making fast progress, perhaps because their native language (L 1) was very different from English, with consequent problems of transfer or interference.

Functional courses often appear to be very steeply graded so far as grammatical items are concerned. This of course is because one function will have several exponents in terms of structure and, in grading their material functionally, material writers will probably select more than one structure for each function. A good example of this is found in *Strategies* (Abbs *et al*, 1975 a) where in the second half of unit 10 the following structures are presented to express the related functions of expressing obligation and necessity in the present and future: *must, have to, don't have to, will have to, have got to, needn't*. Each language item is presented and practised once in a contextualised drill and then practised further in a variety of communicative activities. Students meeting the structures for the first time would probably have difficulty in coping with the variety within such a limited time-scale and would therefore need supplementary exercises to help them learn the language forms. On the other hand, students who had already met the forms *must, have to*, etc. in other contexts and had partly learned them, would benefit greatly from meeting the various ways of expressing obligation and necessity again, consolidating their knowledge of the language form, and, just as importantly, gaining insight into the meanings of these forms which cannot, of course, be used interchangeably in every situation.

This consolidation of knowledge is also referred to as **recycling**. Let us take as an example the teaching of new vocabulary items, or lexis. It is rarely sufficient to introduce a new vocabulary item once only and then forget about it. A word may need to be recycled three, four, five or six times before it is learned adequately. A principle of recycling is that words are best recycled in different contexts. In this way the students learn the form of the word, its sound and its spelling, through progressive exposure to it, and by meeting it in a number of different contexts they develop a fuller understanding of its meaning.

The concept of recycling brings us to our final point here: the difference between **linear progression** and **cyclical progression**. A course with a linear progression, having adopted an order of presentation for each language item, then deals with each item exhaustively before passing on to the next item. The advantage of such an approach is obvious: each new item is thoroughly learned and then forms a sure platform from which the learner can move to the next unfamiliar item. The disadvantage is perhaps less obvious: there is so much to learn in a language that the learner progressing in this fashion may need to spend a considerable amount of time, perhaps even one or two years, before achieving any sort of communicative competence even in relatively uncomplicated situations.

A cyclical course moves fairly quickly from one language item to another and then progressively returns to each item, once, twice or more times, later in the course. The effect of this is that the learner acquires a wider range of expressive possibility in the language at an earlier stage but has not learnt each item as thoroughly as in a linear course. So, although the learner may be less accurate, he has a better-developed ability to communicate.

Provided that students follow their courses to the end, the final result may not be very different whichever kind of progression is used, linear or cyclical. But if a significant number of students leave a course at mid-point for any reason, then a cyclical course may be more suitable as the students who leave will leave with something potentially useful to them.

The two different approaches may also affect learner motivation, particularly at mid-point in the course. One cannot however generalise about this as some learners prefer a slow but thorough and methodical approach whereas others are happier 'flitting' from one item to another and then returning later for a second look. The differences here are both individual and cultural.

When deciding between a linear or a cyclical course we should bear in mind the individual and cultural make-up of our group of learners, the length of the course, its objectives, and whether the students will follow the course to its end. There is a world of difference between a secondary school class for whom education is compulsory and a group of adult learners attending classes in the evenings. The drop-out rate in part-time evening classes can be high, particularly where students feel that they are not getting an immediate return for the very real investment of time and energy that they are making. Such students would most probably benefit from a cyclical approach whereas a class of secondary school pupils following a three, four or even five year course in English leading to a formal examination which stresses accuracy are likely to be taught more effectively following a linear progression.

4 Implications for the evaluation of language teaching materials

I have suggested that the coursebook writer is in effect designing a syllabus as well as producing teaching material, except in the relatively rare instances where a writer organises the course around an existing syllabus. (It should be noted here that most examination 'syllabuses' are not full syllabuses in the sense that I have been using, but are comparable rather with a statement of objectives, whether expressed in functional or structural terms.)

Implicit in coursebooks for language teaching there must be a view of, or an approach to, syllabus design. It is manifested in the language items that the writer selects to teach and in the grading of them. Any coursebook will be permeated with the writer's assumptions about syllabus design, whether they have been explicitly formulated and theoretically justified or simply operate on an intuitive level in the writer's thinking. It is therefore very important that, when setting out to analyse and evaluate teaching material, we should know what options are open to a writer in designing his syllabus.

4.1 Functional and structural syllabuses in practice

If we look at the introductions to some general courses we shall see that, where reference is made to selection and grading, there is some mention of the usefulness of the language being taught. The authors of *Streamline English* (Hartley and Viney, 1978, p. 7) give the following criteria for selection and grading:

> 1. complexity 2. frequency 3. general usefulness 4. immediate usefulness.

These criteria appear to be primarily structural with a secondary level of selection in terms of functions. What seems to happen is that a structural progression is decided upon and the exponents of these structures are made to be as useful, communicatively speaking, as possible. Additionally a number of useful expressions, realisations of particularly useful functions, are taught at various points in the syllabus as formulae, i.e. on a one-off basis as in a phrase book.

So, in *Departures*, the first book of the series, there is a structural progression based essentially on grammatical complexity (although what is meant by complexity is not discussed) with the verb tenses, for example, taught in a conventional sequence: initially the verb *to be* in the present simple form, followed by the present continuous, present simple, past simple, present perfect, and *shall/will* future forms of regular and irregular verbs. Interspersed in this progression are items such as *I'd like ...*, *would you like ...*, and *could you ...*.

Kernel One (O'Neill, 1979) also appears to have a structural base with allowance made for usefulness:

> Kernel One is not a rigidly structural course. It does not try to present grammatical forms simply because they are part of the system, for their own sake. It presents things because they can be seen generally to be useful.

Starting Strategies (Abbs and Freebairn, 1977) takes more of a functional approach, stating in its introduction that:

> this course ... takes as its main starting point for language development what a learner wants to do through language.'

But the authors add that they

> still think it right to grade learning material by taking simple structures before more difficult ones, introducing the present simple before the past tense, simple clauses before complex ones.

The authors of both *Kernel One* and *Starting Strategies* are aware of the danger inherent in the functional approach, of teaching merely phrases or formulae without teaching the structure of the language which alone allows the speaker to use the language creatively, to produce novel utterances and to express his own ideas or feelings. The authors of *Starting Strategies* write that:

> a purely functional course can . . . run the risk of looking rather like a tourist phrase book; the learner may see the immediate application of the language, but will not be given any insight into the way the language works. The result is that he cannot readily create language to suit his needs in different situations.

O'Neill writes in the same vein that:

> *Kernel One* is based on the concept that learners have to learn things in such a way that they can make *independent, creative* use of them. This means that they have to learn a lot more than a collection of useful phrases. They have to acquire things also in a structured, grammatical way.

If we compare the language items introduced in the first ten or fifteen units of a number of modern general English language courses we will see a remarkable similarity in both selection and sequencing. Whether the course is primarily functional or structural seems to make little difference because a structurally-based course today must take account of the insights provided into language use by the functional approach, whilst a functionally-based course cannot ignore the structural complexity of language if it is to be more than a phrase book.

What is perhaps more relevant to our interest than a supposed structural/functional dichotomy is that modern language-teaching materials show an awareness of the fact that there is in language a correspondence of some kind between form and function and that such correspondence is context-dependent. In other words, an appropriate form used to realise a language function in one situation may well be inappropriate in another situation. A language user 'perceives and categorises the social situations of his world and differentiates his ways of speaking accordingly'. (Cazden, 1970).

We have no real description as yet of how the form/function relationship operates in English, but clearly it is central to effective language use and therefore to effective language learning. The native speaker proceeds intuitively and usually successfully, the foreign learner depends on his teacher and coursebook. Coursebooks deal with the problem in an intuitive rather than a systematic way, as each coursebook writer draws on his intuition as a native speaker, but, as I have mentioned above, there is a remarkable similarity between coursebooks, and this suggests that the intuition of the various writers is fairly standard.

There is little empirical information, beyond the collective experience of generations of language teachers, to guide the materials writer in grading grammatical structures in terms of supposed difficulty of learning. Equally there is no objective standard for deciding to teach students how to perform certain kinds of communicative acts rather than others, beyond the writer's own judgement of what the learner is most likely to want to do through language.

Syllabuses then, very much reflect the subjective judgement of their creators whether they are functional or structural. Most these days are to some extent both functional and structural and, at least at the beginner level, show great similarities with one another. Widdowson (1979, p. 250) suggests that 'the work on notional syllabuses can best be seen ... as a means of developing the structural syllabus rather than replacing it'.

4.2 Case study: two courses compared

Contact English (Granger and Hicks, 1977) has a structurally-based progression. This is clear from the contents page and introduction even though it is never stated explicitly in the Teachers' Book. *Starting Strategies* (Abbs and Freebairn, 1977), as we have seen, takes communicative acts, or language functions, as its starting point.

If we compare the language items taught in the first ten units of each course, we find that the following items are taught in both courses:

> *What ... ?*
> *to be* (present simple)
> indefinite and definite articles
> possessives
> numbers
> imperative
> *Would you like ... + noun?* (formula)
> informal greeting and leave-taking

In the second ten units of each course there are still many similarities (present simple, demonstratives, count/non-count nouns, prepositions of place, *would you like* + infinitive) but the differences are more numerous.

The main differences between the first twenty units of each course are that *Contact English* teaches the present continuous whereas *Starting Strategies*, surprisingly perhaps, does not. On the other hand *Starting Strategies* teaches the past simple relatively early, in unit 16, whilst *Contact English* only introduces it in unit 22. The introduction of the past simple in *Starting Strategies* is in no way systematic and does not claim to be so. Quite simply, a few common verbs are given in the past simple form and have to be learnt as individual items: there is no attempt to teach any rule for past tense formation. Although systematic presentation occurs in the next book in the series, *Building Strategies* (Abbs and Freebairn, 1979), this kind of procedure does seem to come uncomfortably close to the kind of phrase book learning that is arguably not true language learning, because the grammatical structure of the language is not being internalised by the student, with the consequence that he is unable to produce sentences of his own making.

Summary

It is important to evaluate the approach to syllabus design adopted by a coursebook. Generally speaking a structural syllabus with a linear progression will be suitable for students who are to pursue a prolonged period of study leading to a high level of performance and accuracy. Secondary school and university courses often fall into this category. On the other hand, a functional syllabus with a cyclical progression is more suitable for adults who are learning English for particular purposes and expect to put what they learn to practical use in the near future.

Structural syllabuses and functional syllabuses need not necessarily be considered as alternatives and the two approaches can be combined by a process of compromise. In certain cases the actual language items taught and their sequence may not differ a lot between a structurally-based course and a functionally-based course. In other cases, however, the differences may be considerable, reflecting different emphases in the books. Identifying the extent of such differences is part of the task of materials evaluation.

Exercises and activities

(a) Look at the way the content of your coursebook is organised (the contents page should be a good indication of this) and decide whether it follows a mainly structural or a mainly functional syllabus. (See section 1 in this chapter.)

(b) Do you feel that the needs of your students/pupils are best met by a structural syllabus or a functional syllabus? (See sections 1 and 2 in this chapter.)

(c) Examine the progression for teaching new language items in your coursebook. Does it follow a linear or a cyclical pattern? Which do you feel is most suitable for your classes? (See page 26.)

(d) Take two coursebooks at the same level (elementary or intermediate), one functional and one structual in approach, and list the language items taught in each book and in what order. What are the main similarities and differences?

4 Presentation and Practice of New Language Items

In this chapter and the next we shall be focusing on some methodological criteria for use in the evaluation process. The methodological views underlying teaching materials may not be explicit, but they will become evident when the materials are examined. Just as a teacher may not expound his methodological procedures when teaching a class, or even when discussing work with colleagues, so a coursebook writer may not discuss in the introduction or Teacher's Book all the rationale which underlies his approach. Indeed so far as the writer is concerned some of the procedures may be more intuitive than explicit.

Whilst I would agree that, as in so much to do with the teaching of language, the whole of a lesson or of a piece of teaching material is greater than the sum total of its parts, it can nevertheless by useful to adopt an analytical approach and identify what methodological assumptions have been made. The analysis of the methodology of a course, whilst not claiming to account for every aspect of that course, does provide valuable insights which allow prospective users to gauge whether the approach of the coursebook writer accords with their own approach and whether in their judgement it is suitable for their students.

1 The influence of theories of learning

1.1 Behaviourist and cognitive views

Language learning had for many years up to the 1960s been seen, albeit in a fairly simplistic way, as a **cognitive activity**, that is to say as an activity which engaged conscious mental processes such as analysing and understanding, and involved learning and applying explicitly formulated rules. The grammar/ translation method which was dominant at that time is essentially cognitive in that it requires a clear understanding of rules and the ability to apply the given rules to new examples of language. The weakness of this method, of course, lies in its too-limited concept of what is involved in learning and using a language. Being able to learn a rule, and then apply it to an academic exercise involving translating sentences (often isolated sentences) from the L1 to the L2 is hardly fully representative of real-life language use in normal situations.

Following grammar/translation in the 1960s, the influence of Skinner and **behaviourist theory** all but revolutionised foreign-language learning with the concept that language learning, like all other learning, is essentially habit formation in response to external stimuli. Thus with a simple stimulus-response-reinforcement sequence, it was claimed learners could develop habits of use in the target language (L2). According to behaviourist thinking it wasn't really necessary for learners to internalise rules; instead they should learn the right patterns of linguistic behaviour, and acquire the correct habits.

That a complex phenomenon like language learning and use should be explained away as a simple process of habit-formation, now seems hard to understand, but language learning and teaching theory in the 1960s was deeply influenced by behaviourism, although it must be said that some writers and teachers, to their credit, remained more than a little sceptical.

In the 1970s there was a gradual moving away from behaviourist-based approaches and a reassertion of cognitive values together with a greater concern for the learner as an individual with well-developed mental faculties and a pre-disposition to learn in an active, searching way. Caleb Gattegno, the initiator of the somewhat controversial Silent Way approach to language teaching, made a very valid point when he expressed his belief that the human being was the most efficient learning organism ever devised (Gattegno, 1976).

The return to a more cognitive approach did not herald a resurgence of grammar/translation based teaching, but did reassert the importance of the psychology of the individual as an autonomous, thinking being worthy of and entitled to respect from his teacher. Indeed, to a considerable extent the emphasis has shifted from language teaching to language learning, the teacher now being seen as the manager of a learning situation. In parallel to this movement, teaching materials have become more sensitive to the individual's learning process and instead of bombarding him with batteries of mechanical drills they now tend to stimulate the learner, to encourage him in his problem-solving activities and to guide the learner in seeking out and putting into use the rules that he is learning.

A full discussion of the behaviourist/cognitive divergence of views is beyond the scope of this book, and is in any case becoming of largely academic interest as the influence of behaviourist psychology wanes. Those who wish to pursue the issue further are referred to Dakin (1973, chapter 2) and Rivers (1968, pp. 71–80).

So far as teaching materials are concerned, those heavily influenced by behaviourist thinking are likely (a) to have been published before 1973, (b) to contain considerable numbers of mechanical drills, many of which could be done by students without understanding what they were saying, (c) not to provide any explanation of the grammar being taught, (d) not to tell the students what they are supposed to be learning and (e) to concentrate heavily on oral work, even to the extent of preventing learners from seeing the written language during the early stages of the course.

1.2 Inductive and deductive language learning

It is useful to distinguish between these two different learning strategies, although it would be wrong to suggest that an individual learner uses only one or the other, or indeed that one is inherently better than the other.

In both types of learning we are concerned with rule formation and use by the learner. The difference springs from the point of entry and the processes involved. In **inductive** learning the learner is presented with a number of examples which embody the rule and by identifying similarities between the examples he hypothesises what he thinks the rule might be and tries it out, seeking confirmation of the hypothesis. This is the way children are thought to acquire their native language, although children, unlike the foreign language learner, will be exposed to fairly random bits of language. The L2 learner is more fortunate in this respect as the examples presented will (or should) be systematic and fully representative of the rule which is to be learned. The essential point here is that, from examples of language, the learner **induces** the rule and then uses it.

In **deductive** learning, the process works in reverse: the learner is given an explanation of the rule in an analytical way and is then expected to apply the rule and provide his own instances of language, perhaps guided by an example or two.

The desired end product is the same: the ability to use the rules of the language both productively and receptively. It is only the route taken in attaining this objective that differs.

Let us suppose that you wish to teach negative question tags in the present tense on the model:

You like oranges, don't you?

Teaching inductively, or to be more precise, getting your students to learn inductively, you would present several examples which followed the same model, e.g.

You live in Brighton, don't you?
You travel to school by train, don't you?
You study in the mornings, don't you?
You have lunch with your friends at the Cat & Fiddle, don't you? etc.

and then encourage your students to produce their own examples based on the model. You hope that your students will have worked out for themselves, perhaps intuitively, the rule for this particular structure, and that they will be able to use it, given sufficient practice. So you may ask members of the class to say things about what their classmates do regularly (therefore using the simple present) and to add a question tag seeking confirmation.

Using a deductive approach, you would first explain the rule in an explicit way, along the lines 'To form a question tag, you must use the auxiliary verb *do* in the same tense as the main verb in the sentence but in the interrogative form. If the main verb is affirmative, the tag verb is negative, and vice-versa.' Then you may give a couple of examples to make the rule clearer. This would be followed by some sentences without question tags and the students would be required to provide the correct tag in each case. Essentially this kind of exercise is a test to see if the students can operate the rule that they have (or are supposed to have) learnt. From the rule, the students are meant to **deduce** correct instances of language.

Either route to learning is acceptable, and often the sequence of inductive learning reinforced by deductive learning (i.e. trying to work out the rule first and then having it given) proves to be the most effective, particularly with adults. Children learn inductively better than adults, whilst adults, having better developed analytical capacities, can better understand and use abstract rules. We should never hinder our students' learning by holding dogmatically and exclusively to one strategy or the other. Teaching is a pragmatic process and we should use whatever method brings the best results.

What we must ensure is that a real language-learning process, in the full sense of the word, is taking place when our students go through the motions of learning sentences, dialogues etc. They must be able to use creatively the rules that they have learned so as to meet their own needs and satisfy their own purposes.

2 Presentation and practice of grammar items

2.1 Presentation of new structures

The way in which language items are presented in a coursebook can vary considerably, and so far we have looked at the difference between an inductive and a deductive learning strategy. We are now going to look at how course material actually presents and gives practice in using grammar items (structures).

How are new structures presented? To what extent is the presentation related to what has been previously learned? Is it meaningful (in context), systematic, representative of the underlying grammar rule, appropriate to the given context, relevant to learners' needs and interests? Are the practice activities for new structures adequate in number, varied, meaningful?

Presentation is the initial stage of learning a new item. The teacher provides the new information, the new piece of knowledge, and the learner concentrates on understanding it and remembering it. Although he may not seem to be doing very much overtly at this stage, the learner is in fact very active mentally as he seeks to understand and internalise the new rule which is being presented.

At the **practice stage**, the second stage of learning a new item, the learner starts to use the new language item, at first in carefully controlled exercises, which give a good deal of help and prevent the learner from making too many mistakes. The degree of control can be lessened as the learner becomes more confident.

The free **production stage** is the final stage and here the student is helped to use the language that he has learned in uncontrolled activities which are modelled on those of real life. The student is now being prepared for using English in the world outside the classroom. Free production will be covered in Chapter 5.

Learning a new item is facilitated if the learner can relate it, through similarity, comparison or contrast, with what is already familiar. In the foreign language learning situation this relationship could be established with the native language (L1) or with what is already known of the foreign language (L2) or it could be established with something non-linguistic, such as a picture, an object, an action or a sound. Course materials may use any or all of these procedures to structure and contextualise the learning process.

Let us consider the relationship with what is already known of the L2. Obviously this is impossible with complete 'zero' beginners in which case a link with a non-linguistic element is more likely. (Most courses at the beginner level begin by presenting a number of vocabulary items linked to pictures and occurring in simple declarative sentences with the verb *to be*.) However, once the learner has even a limited competence in English it is possible and desirable that new language items should be presented in relationship with what is already known. The relationship is usually one of contrast or of comparison, where similarities and differences are noted.

As language is a highly-structured, inter-related system it is imperative that language items should be learned not in isolation but in relation to each other. This applies equally to grammar and vocabulary. Presented in a relationship of comparison, language items tend to define one another in terms of what they do mean and what they do not mean, and of where they can be used appropriately and where they cannot be used. It is after all just as important to know what a structure or a word doesn't mean as to know what it does mean. In point of fact one cannot know the full range of meaning of an item without also knowing the limits of that range of meaning.

The teaching of verb tenses often relies on comparing the form and meaning of a new tense with the tenses which have already been learned. For instance, the present simple tense, used to refer to a regular or habitual action, can be compared with the present continuous used to describe an action taking place now, e.g.

> The 7.30 train to Manchester is now leaving platform 3.
> The 7.30 train to Manchester always leaves from platform 3.

Similarly the meaning of the present perfect form of the verb (usually a big difficulty for students) can be taught in a context which contrasts it with the past simple (see p. 69 for a practical example of this).

In vocabulary teaching, let us consider the word *cottage*. Now, one way of teaching *cottage* would be to show one or more pictures of cottages, and I suppose that most of us would opt for a chocolate-box thatched black-and-white building for an example. This is not an unacceptable procedure, but one could teach the meaning of *cottage* more fully by relating it to other words already known by the students which refer to different kinds of buildings. If we do this we will be using for teaching purposes the lexical patterning, or semantic structure of the lexicon of English and consequently providing our learners with insights into this structured system.

Supposing the students already know the following lexical items: building, house, palace, castle, flat, hotel, town-house, then cottage can be presented as a kind of house which in its turn is a kind of building. A cottage however is unlike certain other kinds of building: it is not a palace because it is too small and too modest; it is not a castle because it is not defensive and again it is too small; it is not a flat because it lies on its own patch of ground; it is not a hotel because it is used as a private residence and is, again, too small; it is not a town house because it is usually situated in the country either in an isolated position or in a village. We have thus established that a cottage is small, modest, and usually situated in a rural environment. In this way our learners have developed a concept which they can link to the word, and which is not limited to the one visual instance of a thatched black-and-white building that we may have been tempted to show them. If students were only shown the standard picture of a cottage, one wonders what they would make of references to rows of miners' cottages in a pit village in Nottinghamshire. The visual images conjured up could be quite bizarre!

We should therefore look very carefully at our course material and see what sort of relationships are established between the familiar and the new.

The presentation of structure should be coherent and systematic so that the learners can readily perceive the pattern and hence the rule underlying the models given. The models, or examples, themselves should of course be typical of and representative of the rule being taught. Presenting the comparison of adjectives in such a way that the following five examples occur – *dimmer, greyer, freer, prettier, more exciting* – will have the effect of teaching the student five individual instances of comparatives but will not allow the student to perceive the underlying rules with any certainty because in the written medium five different forms are being presented and in the spoken medium two different forms. The examples are not presented systematically enough for the student to be able to generalise from the individual instances given.

Presentation models should be appropriate to the context in which they occur. Without demanding total realism, we have a right to expect the presentation models to be acceptable as exponents of communicative functions. In other words we need to be able to believe that what is presented could be used for a communicative purpose and is not included as language for language's sake. Many coursewriters experience difficulty in realistically contextualising the very early stages of learning English, and sequences such as the following are commonplace:

Bob	This is a fish.
Mrs Gray	Is this a fish?
Bob	Yes, it is. And that's a fish too.
Bob	This is a cat.
Mrs Gray	Is this a cat?
Bob	Yes, it is. And that's a cat too.

(Benhamou and Dominique, *Speak English* (Nathan, 1972))

Bob, a small boy, has drawn pictures of two fishes, two cats etc. which are well represented visually in the coursebook, and he is talking about his drawing with Mrs Gray.

Such an exchange is not wholly authentic, and is perhaps not quite realistic enough to be acceptable. The following drill from a coursebook in use in China also seems to me to be less than acceptable because, as a piece of practice material, it generates sentences which would simply not occur. Even in China mothers are not employed as soldiers and coal miners, and the implied expectation that husband and wife probably do the same job in each case is unnatural. The lexical items in lines 5–8 are, of course, supposed to be substituted for the items in italics in lines 1–4.

> – What does your father do?
> – He's a *doctor*.
> – Is your mother a *doctor*, too?
> – No, she isn't. She's a *nurse*.
>
> a soldier, a barefoot doctor;
> a cadre, a bus driver;
> a school teacher, a steel worker;
> a coal miner, an office worker.

English 1 (Beijing Languages Institute, 1979)

It has become fashionable to criticize the teaching of the present continuous form of the verb by associating it with a number of simultaneous actions such as '*I'm sitting down*', '*I'm standing up*', '*I'm walking to the door*', on the grounds that if the students can see the activity they do not need to be given a commentary on it, and therefore the model is presented in a context which could never occur in real life. Ingenious teachers have overcome the difficulty by blindfolding a student and then getting other students to give the commentary! This, it is claimed, overcomes the difficulty and makes the language used communicative. Such contrived situations however could hardly be called authentic and although the interaction may be communicative, the context of situation could hardly be called realistic.

So long as it is evident that the instances of language being taught have a communicative potential, it is, I suggest, of relatively lesser importance whether or not, at the presentation and practice stages, activities are actually and genuinely communicative and realistic. We have to accept the fact that any teaching or training situation will be artificial to some degree, and necessarily so. In the language classroom, the language items to be learned are selected and presented in a structured and graded manner quite unlike any kind of real-life language use. This is not only acceptable but essential for effective language learning to take place. So long as the final objective is communicative ability and this objective is not lost to sight, then we should not worry too much if some of the learning processes, which are after all only a means to an end, seem a little artificial.

I am not of course arguing for artificiality for its own sake and would prefer realism where it is possible to achieve it. A good example is this neat presentation of the present continuous:

Helen	Who's in the bathroom? Is that you David?
David	Yes.
Helen	What are you doing? I'm waiting.
David	I'm brushing my teeth.
Helen	Quick, please. We're late.
David	All right!
Helen	David, please! What are you doing now?
David	I'm washing my hair.
Helen	Now? You're not washing your hair now!
David	My hair is dirty.
Helen	It's half past seven! Mummy!
Mrs Gray	David! Open that door! Quick.
David	Yes, Mummy.
Mrs Gray	David! What are you doing?
Helen	Look! He isn't washing his hair, he's playing with his boat! And I'm waiting!

(Benhamou and Dominique, *Speak English* (Nathan 1972))

Here we have a realistic dialogue set in a perfectly acceptable context: a situation where one speaker does not know what the other is doing and wants to find out. Moreover the purpose in using the present continuous here is not simply to elicit information. Helen is trying to get David to do something and is using language to that purpose. It is therefore an example of language use presented as purposeful behaviour, and as such can be readily accepted as relevant to the learner's potential communicative needs.

2.2 Practice activities for new structures

Activities for language practice range from mechanical, automatic drilling at one extreme to guided role-play at the other. One characteristic of practice activities is that they provide the learner with the opportunity to use what has already been presented and to use it in a controlled learning situation where the likelihood of error is reduced. Under the most tightly controlled conditions the possibility of error is almost nil, as in this example of a drill (the left-hand column is the prompt and the right-hand column the student's response):

some bread	– May I have some bread, please? –
some fruit	– May I have some fruit, please? –
a little ice	– May I have a little ice, please? –
a little butter	– May I have a little butter, please? –
some salt	– May I have some salt, please? –
a little wine	– May I have a little wine, please? –

(J.A. Barnett, *Success with English Tapescripts 1* (Penguin, 1968))

In this particular drill, so long as the student substitutes the new item accurately, he is in no danger of making a mistake. Such drills are useful for developing quick, automatic responses, particularly where formulaic expressions are involved or where there is very limited syntactic choice, as in the formation of question tags. The danger is that they can be done quite accurately by students who have no understanding of the meaning of what they are saying. Another, more insidious, danger is that the students will understand what they are saying in literal terms but will not grasp the value of the sentence as a communicative act. In other words they will understand the structure but not its function. In the example given above the student may well believe that he is asking a question, as the sentence is in the interrogative form. There is nothing in the drill which indicates that he is in fact making a request.

It is of course unfair to consider an individual drill in isolation: it should be viewed as part of a teaching/learning sequence and if it is appropriately used it can be perfectly acceptable. If this drill is used, the meaning and function of the sentence should have been taught beforehand and afterwards one would expect to see a progression to less controlled exercises which allow the student more freedom of choice.

Open dialogues or one-sided dialogues give the student a certain amount of choice, within a structured activity. In the example below each student is given one part of a dialogue and practices it with a partner who has the other part. The dialogues, although fairly fixed, do offer some scope for individual choice, such as the selection of items from the menu, a copy of which is given to each student in the pair.

---

10   One-sided dialogue: at a restaurant

Read the following dialogue with Student B.

Unfortunately, you can only see your part, so you will have to listen very carefully to what Student B says. Use the menu on the next page.

Before starting, read through your part to get an idea of what the dialogue is all about.

You:	It's a nice restaurant, don't you think?
Student B:	......
You:	No, not really. What about you?
Student B:	......
You:	Oh, I see. Now, let's have a look at the menu. (*slight pause*) What would you like to start with?

Student B: ......
    You: Yes, I think I'll have the same. No, on second thoughts, I'll have...... (*name a dish*).
Student B: ......
    You: Well, I don't like...... (*repeat dish*) very much, actually. I think I'd prefer...... (*name another dish*). I had it the last time I was here and it was really delicious.
Student B: ......
    You: Yes, good. And what about some vegetables with the meal?
Student B: ......
    You: Yes, let's see. (*slight pause*) I think I'll have...... (*name two vegetables*).
Student B: ......
    You: Right. Now, where's the waiter?

10   One-sided dialogue: at a restaurant

Read the following dialogue with Student A.
    Unfortunately, you can only see your part, so you will have to listen very carefully to what Student A says. Use the menu on the next page.
    Before starting, read through your part to get an idea of what the dialogue is all about.

Student A: ......
    Yes: Yes, very nice indeed. You come here often, then?
Student A: ......
    You: Oh no! I've only been here once before, actually. That was...... (*say when it was*).
Student A: ......
    You: Well, I wouldn't mind...... (*name a dish*). What about you?
Student A: ......
    You: Right. And what shall we have for the main course? The ...... (*name a dish*) sounds rather nice.
Student A: ......
    You: Oh, in that case, I'll have...... (*repeat the dish*) too.
Student A: ......
    You: Well, let's see what's on the menu.
Student A: ......
    You: Yes ... that sounds good for me as well. I'll order the same.
Student A: ......

Fig. 4. (Watcyn-Jones, *Pair Work* (Penguin, 1981))

The main principle to bear in mind when using controlled practice material is to select exercises which exert sufficient control over the student's production to avoid excessive error, but to use no more control than is necessary. Course-books should ideally contain a variety of exercises with different degrees of control, beginning for each new language item taught with tightly controlled exercises and progressing through a gradual relaxation of control until the student is given a good deal of freedom in making his individual choices. The student should ultimately be brought to a point where he can select appropriately and accurately from the options open at any point in the formulation of discourse. The student should be aware of the options which are open to him and of the implications for future options of each choice that he makes, since as one progresses through a conversational exchange the number of options tends to diminish and later options are largely determined by earlier choices.

3 Presentation and practice of lexis

I have already referred to ways in which we can exploit the lexical patterning which occurs in English. We will now look briefly at ways in which new lexis (vocabulary) can be presented. It can occur in word lists, in association with visuals and in a text (usually a reading passage, although it could occur in a listening text).

Lists of words, unless they are related words, are difficult to learn because the words appear in isolation and, lacking any context, do not appear to the learner to have any meaning. Meaning could possibly be supplied by translation, but this is often impracticable unless course material is designed with speakers of a particular language in mind. In any case, translation tends to give learners the false impression that there are exact one-to-one equivalents between words in English and in their native language. Many learners approach a foreign language believing that it is a coded version of their own language and that all they need to do is to learn the words in the foreign language which correspond to those in their own language and then string them together in the same way. To base one's teaching on translation, unless it is done in a very sophisticated way, risks reinforcing this basic misconception about the relationships between languages.

Presenting new lexis in association with visuals, or in a text, has the built-in advantage that the words are encountered in a context, whether non-linguistic (visuals) or linguistic (texts). Context makes meaning clearer and in many cases allows students to deduce the meaning of new and unfamiliar words by informed guessing. Therefore in our course material we should look for the presentation of lexis in a meaningful context of one sort or another.

A word is not learned as soon as it has been met and understood. It should be recycled by being introduced subsequently in a number of different contexts, productively as well as receptively.

The amount of new lexis to be taught in any one unit is a debatable point, but as a rule of thumb, the number of new words in a text should not amount to more than about five percent of the total. So in a 300 word text up to fifteen new words could be introduced.

4 Phonology

Many general courses tend to ignore **phonology** (the sound system) altogether, or else just teach **pronunciation** in an incidental fashion, perhaps as an offshoot of a structure drill. I have earlier pointed out the difficulty of integrating a graded presentation of the sound system into a general course, which also has to be carefully graded in its grammar and vocabulary. Nevertheless, in a general course one would expect to see some attention paid to the teaching of pronunciation in its own right.

Out of four of the most widely used beginners' courses at the time of writing, only two deal explicitly with any aspects of phonology. *Kernel One* (O'Neill, 1979) provides models for stress and intonation in the Teacher's Book and contains practice exercises. *Starting Strategies* (Abbs and Freebairn, 1977) provides material in the teacher's notes and in the tapescript for both articulation of individual sounds and for stress and intonation. *Contact English 1* (Granger and Hicks, 1977) and *Streamline English-Departures* (Hartley and Vlney, 1978) do not make any explicit reference either to the articulation of sounds or to stress and intonation.

Intonation is an extremely powerful device in speech and usually overrides grammar and vocabulary so far as meaning is concerned. Consider for example how a declarative sentence such as *You're coming* can be assigned the value of a question simply through the use of an intonation pattern with a rising tone. The grammatical structure remains unchanged yet the meaning is completely altered. Similarly *yes* in answer to a question, spoken with a fall-rise tone, will normally have the meaning *no* as in this example:

A John's a nice fellow, isn't he?
B Yes, but don't you think he's a bit moody?

In view of the evident power of intonation as a device in speech, it may seem a little odd that some very reputable courses do not attempt to teach it, except in the most oblique way.

If you should find yourself using such a course, all is not lost, as you can turn to some of the excellent supplementary material for teaching pronunciation which is now on the market and integrate it into your teaching programme. For **sound production and recognition** there is *Sound Right!* (Mortimer, 1975) and for teaching **stress**: *Stress Time* (Mortimer, 1976). Some of the commoner intonation patterns of English can be taught with *Using Intonation* (Cook, 1979). Another useful book for pronunciation teaching is *Ship or Sheep?* (Baker, 1977). These books are suitable for use with lower intermediate level students and above.

One feature which is shared by these books is the presentation of phonological features, whether they are individual sounds, stress patterns or intonation contours, in a systematic way. Additionally, the presentation and practice material consists largely of dialogues which provide context and consequently meaning. This is particularly important where intonation is concerned. It is as pointless to learn the form of an **intonation contour**, such as **rise-fall**, without learning its meaning, as it is to learn the form of a word such as *tablecloth* without knowing what is referred to. Where the articulation of individual sounds, or **phonemes**, is concerned, there is little to motivate the student if he is asked to intone apparently meaningless sounds in isolation. However, when they form part of an interesting or amusing dialogue, the learning process comes alive as it takes on meaning and acquires a purpose.

In integrating this pronunciation-teaching material into a general course, particularly at elementary level, great care must be taken not to use pronunciation exercises which include structures or vocabulary which are too difficult for the learners. We should, as far as possible, only teach one thing at a time and we should avoid at all costs finding ourselves in the position of having to teach in an ad hoc fashion a new grammatical structure that happens to crop up in a pronunciation exercise.

Summary

At the presentation stage, great care has to be taken to present examples of English which are fully representative of the underlying rule which is to be learned. At the practice stage, drills and exercises should be controlled so that students do not make too many errors, but the amount of control should be the minimum necessary to avoid excessive error. As the students progress, greater scope should be allowed for them to make their own choices. In both presentation and practice, language items should be meaningful. Meaning can be taught through context, both linguistic context and non-linguistic context.

We should look for systematic, ordered presentation and practice not only of structures, but also of vocabulary and pronunciation. Where the sound system of English is not taught, or only sketchily dealt with in a general course, then the teacher should look for suitable supplementary material and integrate it into the teaching programme.

Exercises and activities

(a) Take a reading passage or dialogue in your coursebook and count the number of new vocabulary items in it. Express the number of new words as a percentage of the total number of words in the passage. Do you consider this to be a high or a low percentage? (See page 40).

(b) Choose three exercises giving controlled practice in a structure of English. The exercises can practise the same structure or different structures. Put them in order according to the degree of control which is exercised over the students' choice and identify how that control is achieved (e.g. by the use of a substitution table, by visual cues, etc.). What sort of communicative activities do you think that the exercise could be used to prepare the student for? (See question 4.2.2 in Chapter 10.)

(c) Does your coursebook include material for teaching intonation patterns? If YES, how is it done? Are you satisfied with it? If NO, can you find supplementary material which can be integrated into your teaching programme? (See question 4.4 in Chapter 10.)

5 Developing Language Skills and Communicative Abilities

Being able to communicate effectively in English means being proficient in the various language skills involved in the communication process, but it means more than being able to perform in each of the four skills separately. It also means being able to use the skills effectively in various combinations depending on the nature of the interaction. Conversation, for instance, involves speaking and listening skills, not independent of each other but in very close combinations.

1 Free production of spoken English

By free production of spoken English I mean the use of English in an uncontrolled situation. This must be the goal of language teaching and by the gradual reduction of control in exercises we should bring our learners to the point where they can use English in an autonomous fashion for their own purposes. It is clearly not enough to stop the learning process when the student is able to perform adequately in controlled drilling. The student must be given practice in (and be exposed to models of) the communicative strategies necessary for effective communication. In a conversation, for instance, it is not sufficient simply to produce grammatically correct sentences. The sequence of sentences used must link together and show a coherent development. The speakers need to be able to communicate their attitudes through choice of vocabulary and structure and use of an appropriate tone of voice.

At present not enough is known of the patterns of interaction involved for us to be able to provide an explicit and analytical description of the processes. Research work in progress in fields like ethnomethodology (the study of how people take part in conversations in everyday settings) and discourse analysis may in the future give us a much clearer understanding of what is involved. In the meantime however we can make a very useful practical contribution to our learners' communicative abilities by reproducing, or simulating, in the classroom the sort of situations that students will encounter in the world outside.

There are various techniques for doing this, including role-play, simulation, dramatic activities and games of different kinds. Some general courses include suggestions for these activities at the end of each unit, but others do not. There is, in any case, a good range of specialised materials available in published form, which can be used with students of different levels.

It is important to look at the relative proportion of material for **presentation, practice** and **free production**. Too much emphasis on presentation and controlled practice means that the coursebook will not adequately prepare the student for the real world, whilst lack of attention to clear presentation of grammar in favour of lots of communicative activities may mean that the student will never get a firm grounding in the basics of English.

We should be looking for a balance and a clear progression towards independence on the part of the student. It should be clear that the coursebook ultimately brings students to a point where they can use English on their own and for their own purposes.

2 Materials for reading, listening and writing

Teaching material for these activities is, again, sometimes integrated into general courses and sometimes not.

2.1 Reading

There is plenty of reading material available on the market and many publishers include series of carefully graded readers in their lists. The *Longman Structural Readers* series, for example, has readers graded in terms of grammar and vocabulary into six stages, stage one containing a limited range of structures and a basic vocabulary of some 300 words and stage six containing a wide range of structures and a basic vocabulary of about 1,800 words. The principles of using graded readers are well set out in the *Longman Structural Readers Handbook* and the *Longman Guide to Graded Readers*.

The *Heinemann Guided Readers* series involves control not only of structure and vocabulary but also of information content. The length and complexity of the stories, the number of characters and the background setting are all carefully controlled. As the handbook to the series explains:

> In order to read a book successfully, students are involved in a process of absorbing a stream of information from the printed pages in front of them. In the Heinemann Guided Readers Series, the controlling of this stream of information – making sure that it flows smoothly and evenly and that it can be easily absorbed by the students – is given priority over all other forms of control.

(J. Milne, *Heinemann Guided Readers Handbook* (Heinemann Educational Books, 1977))

Some Readers have accompanying cassettes so that students can listen, or listen and read at the same time. This may appear on the surface to be a useful way of integrating listening and reading skills, and indeed up to a point it is. What must be born in mind however is that the language of these graded readers is written language, and if it is recorded on cassette it is really written English which has been read aloud and recorded. It will not display many of the features of spontaneous speech – such as hesitation, repetition and uncompleted sentences – and it will not incorporate the patterns of interaction which occur in conversation.

2.2 Listening

When looking at listening material we should ask ourselves what sort of listening practice our students need (monologue, dialogue, etc.) and what they are required to do in response to what they hear. Comprehension questions are useful for checking understanding, particularly if they are of the type which requires students to actively seek out the answer and formulate it themselves rather than simply repeat a section of the text. This of course applies equally to comprehension questions on reading passages. Another possible activity is to ask students to identify the purpose of the text and of various parts of it. An advertisement, for instance, will have the purpose of persuading people perhaps to buy a product or perform an action.

Listening activities are often under-represented in general courses and this is a pity because in our own language we almost certainly spend more time listening than doing anything else. Also, as we have seen, listening is an integral part of conversation. Oral skills without equally well-developed listening abilities are of little practical value. We should therefore look for a considerable amount of listening practice in a good course. If it is simply not provided, then we should supplement the course by using some of the specialised listening material on the market.

2.3 Writing

So far as writing exercises are concerned, we should be sensitive to the fact that writing has its own rules and conventions and we can expect course material to take that into account. Writing is not speech written down, and writing ability cannot be adequately taught by simply getting students to write down oral drills or do written grammar exercises. This may help them with their spelling but it will not equip them to produce coherent written text following the conventions of writing. We should look for specific writing exercises which in the earlier stages of learning are based upon given models of written English.

Learners can become aware of the nature of written text by reading and, as I have suggested above, we can help to develop their awareness by focusing their attention on significant features of the text. The next stage is to get our students to write a short, controlled text themselves, based on the model given but containing different information. Here is a good example of an integrated reading and writing exercise:

Exercise 6

Martin's friend, Tom, is a newspaper reporter. When he had been in his job for only one week, his boss told him to write a report about two ships. The news had just arrived to say that the two ships had gone down. The boss wrote a few words on a piece of paper and gave it to Tom with an old report to help him. Here is the old newspaper report and the paper Tom's boss gave him. When you have read them both, write Tom's report for him.

> Last night there was an accident in the mouth of the Thames, when two ships went down. The smaller ship, the *White Rose*, had been going from London to Rotterdam. The other, the *Lady of Lisbon*, had been coming to London from Japan. The *White Rose* had been carrying bicycles and six passengers. The bigger ship had been bringing electrical equipment. Both ships had been travelling slowly and showing the usual lights. Before they went down, a third ship took all the people off, and later brought them to London.

From London to Singapore,
carrying cars,
going slowly.

From Abadan to London,
carrying oil, going quickly,
doing this for 5 years.

Both showing usual lights, all men safe.

Fig. 5. (From *Success with English, Coursebook 2* by G. Broughton (Penguin))

Note how the exercise becomes progressively more difficult as the new information is incorporated into the text. At the beginning it is a process of simple substitution, but by the end of the text some syntactic changes are necessary as well.

If we are evaluating a general course we should certainly ask ourselves, as in the case of phonology, to what extent listening, reading and writing are presented and practised, how thoroughly and systematically this is done, and whether the particular characteristics of each activity are adequately represented.

3 Integrated skills and communicative abilities

I have mentioned earlier that in actual language use we rarely use one skill in isolation. We may of course do so when we are listening to the radio or watching television or when reading a book or newspaper. However even when reading a newspaper or book it is by no means uncommon to read out or paraphrase a short article or extract, or comment on a newspaper story to someone sitting nearby. That person is likely to respond with at the very least a brief comment to acknowledge what has been said. So, a straightforward reading activity may well involve speaking and understanding speech as associated activities. A student reading a textbook may well make notes on the significant points of what he is reading, here combining reading skills with writing skills.

When listening to the radio or watching television I may turn to the *Radio Times* or *TV Times* and read a synopsis of the programme that I am watching. I may even read quite a long article about the programme which will provide me with background information helping me to predict and better understand what I am seeing and hearing. In this case listening skills are complemented by reading skills.

Numerous other communicative situations in real life involve integrating two or more of the four skills. Consider, for example, taking a message over the telephone, taking part in any sort of conversation, filling in a form, writing an abstract of an article, and taking notes from a talk or lecture. In all these situations, and in many more, the user of the language exercises his abilities in two or more skills, either simultaneously or in close succession.

Less obvious, because they do not fall into the category of observable behaviour, are the cognitive processes which relate, or mediate, between the language skills. In a conversation, for instance, speaking and listening are obviously not separate, unrelated activities which happen to occur at the same time and in the same place. What one participant in the conversation says will to some extent be determined by what he hears from the other participants and also by his purpose in joining in the conversation. The next utterance in a conversation is never wholly predictable, unless it consists entirely of an exchange of standard formulae such as 'Good morning' – 'Good morning' or 'Nice day' – 'Yes, isn't it?' We can predict up to a point what can come next or at least we can discount implicitly many unlikely occurrences such as, 'Shall I meet you at the station?' – 'Two coffees please.' This element of prediction of response to within a limited range of possibilities seems to be important in the ability to keep up a sustained conversation, but equally important is the ability to make real-time (spontaneous) responses to utterances which are not wholly predictable. This ability to receive, understand and process a message and respond to it without hesitation is perhaps what we mean when we talk about fluency in language use and it depends to a considerable degree on unseen mental processes.

When looking at course materials which claim to be communicative or to teach integrated skills, we might ask ourselves firstly to what extent the practice material represents real language use and secondly how far development of the cognitive processes referred to above will be helped by using the material.

If we consider a standard procedure for presentation and practice in course-books – the **dialogue** – we shall see that it practises integrated skills: listening, speaking, and, usually, reading. It also appears to be communicative, super-ficially, in that it involves two people in talking to each other in what seems to be a realistic way. Dialogues are certainly useful for presenting new items of language and for practising them in a mechanical fashion, but if we look at them carefully we shall see that they are not fully representative of real language use, nor do they require the student to engage in the same cognitive processes as take place in a conversation.

Although dialogues give practice in listening and speaking, the exchanges are fixed and predetermined as each dialogue has been written, and perhaps also recorded on tape, during the preparation of the coursebook. In taking part in a dialogue the students either read the parts from the book, or repeat them from a tape, or both. This process of reading or repetition, although useful for pronun-ciation practice and the psychomotor function of stringing sounds and words together in English, is not modelled on the processes that occur during a real conversation. There is little or no unpredictability, the direction and content of the conversation are determined in advance, and no genuine communication of any kind takes place as the participants are not using English in any purposeful communicative activity. They are using English in order to use (and practise) English, and, although this inward-looking, circular activity has its place in language learning, it cannot by any stretch of the imagination be accepted as the final objective or end-product of a language-learning programme.

The cognitive processes involved in reading or repeating a dialogue are equally unrepresentative of those which occur in real communicative situations. The process for a written dialogue is one of reading silently and understanding (fully or partially), perhaps listening to it read by the teacher or on tape, and then reading one part aloud, on cue. There is no real response to the other participant and beyond recognising the cue it is not necessary to understand what he says. The real-life sequence of processing a relatively unpredictable message and responding to it by formulating the response in real time (and in the case of con-versation this means almost simultaneously) is lacking.

Some published dialogues offer the possibility of variation through the substitution of different vocabulary items or even short sentences either on cue from the teacher or at the student's will. Here is an example of this procedure. Having introduced different ways of making suggestions and given some relatively free practice, the author invites the readers to practise the following dialogue:

> A　*Why don't we* get ourselves a new car? The old one's
> 　　falling apart. (*Let's . . .*)
> B　Oh, what a good idea!
> A　What kind shall we get?
> B　We *could* look at an MG this time, if you liked. (*might*)
> A　Yes, fine.
> B　When shall we go and look?

A *Why not* sometime next week? (*Why don't we go*)
B No, let's go on Saturday.
A O.K.
B Where shall we go?
A There's a car dealer down the road. *How about* going there? (*What about*)
B No, I don't like that place. *Why don't* we try the garage Martin recommended? (*I suggest . . .*)
A Fine. We'll do that.

(From *Survival English* by J. de Freitas (Macmillan))

However, despite the number of options open to the participants in the dialogue it really *makes no difference* which option is chosen and B's response is the same whether A says 'Why don't we get ourselves a new car' or 'Let's get ourselves a new car'. B still doesn't have to listen to A in order to perform adequately. De Freitas quite rightly points out that 'it should not be thought that the situation (in the dialogue) is any more than one of innumerable settings that could be used to contextualise the language. The learner will understand that he might have to 'defend' himself in all sorts of unforeseeable situations and that linguistic adjustments might be necessary.' Unfortunately the dialogues do not equip the learner to cope with unforeseeable situations because he is locked within the fixed sequence of the dialogue. If the learner has paid attention, he knows how it is going to end before he says the first word. Some suggestions on how to adapt dialogues to make them more representative of real communication will be given in Chapter 9.

This leads us naturally on to consider **discourse**: the combining and relating of sentences and utterances to produce units of language which are sequenced in a structured way. There are clearly rules and conventions by which sentences relate to each other and form larger units, such as a paragraph or a text. These rules are not the same as rules of grammar, and are the subject of continuing research. Course materials should, implicitly or explicitly, bring students to a point where they can operate in English above sentence level. In other words, the aim of a course should not simply be to teach the learner to write or say grammatically correct sentences, but also to develop an awareness of how sentences are organised together in English for communicative purposes.

A very good example of coursebook presentation at this level of sophistication, with particular reference to the development of academic reading abilities, is provided by the series *Reading and Thinking in English* (Oxford University Press, 1979) and in particular the third stage of the series, *Discovering Discourse*. Here students are taught how to recognise the functions of significant parts of a text, such as generalisation, description and classification, together with the formal features which identify them as such.

A description of some of the features of the organisation of English above the level of the sentence is to be found in chapter ten of *A Grammar of Contemporary English* (Quirk et al, 1972) and in chapter ten of *A University Grammar of English* (Quirk and Greenbaum, 1973). Either chapter will repay study in whole or in part.

Summary

Much practice material in EFL courses is tightly controlled and somewhat mechanical – necessarily so as learners cannot be expected to manipulate large quantities of language in the early stages of learning. What we need to look for in coursebooks is whether the practice material stops at the stage where language practice is there for language practice's sake or whether it is recognised that this is only a transitional stage before the learner achieves some degree of communicative competence: the ability to use language for his own purpose, appropriately and confidently.

In order to achieve a degree of communicative ability, the learner needs practice in coping with communicative situations involving the realistic integration of language skills and the development of cognitive strategies, e.g. how to deal with the problem of real-time responses and unpredictability in normal conversation. Communicative activities in the classroom do not have to be totally authentic, indeed any training or learning situation is to some extent artificially contrived, but they must be *representative* of and *modelled* on the processes that take place in real language use.

Exercises and activities

(a) Note the different skills and combinations of skills that you use in your own language over the space of a few hours. Compare your results with the patterns of skills represented in language production activities in your coursebook. Do you feel that the coursebook activities are a good preparation for your students to use English communicatively? (See question 5.3.1 in Chapter 10.)

(b) Take a listening passage from a general course or a specialised book for teaching listening skills and look at the different kinds of exercises linked to it. What is the purpose of each exercise? Which do you think is most useful? (See question 5.2.2 in Chapter 10.)

6 Supporting Materials

Depending on how comprehensive a course is, it may provide some or all of the following: visual material; recorded (taped) material; a teacher's book; an index of grammatical items, functions etc.; a vocabulary list; tests.

1 Visual material, tapes and other aids for the teacher

1.1 Visual material

Visual material includes pictures in the coursebook, flashcards, wall charts, film strips, slides, videotapes and even 16mm sound film. Effective visuals should be usable: it should be possible to teach with them and through them. It is very important to distinguish between visuals which can be used for teaching an item such as a new verb form (e.g. visuals depicting a series of actions in progress and then completed) and visuals which serve only as illustrations, to make the page look more attractive, and do not form an integral part of the teaching material. It is usually easy to distinguish between the two, as in the former case exercises and other activities will direct the students' attention to the appropriate visuals and require a verbal response based on information provided visually. An example of a visual which is largely illustrative is reproduced in Figure 6 below, and an example of visuals which are integral to the course and are an essential part of the teaching material is shown in Figure 7 opposite.

---

40 Food and Talk

Last week at a dinner-party, the hostess asked me to sit next to Mrs Rumbold. Mrs Rumbold was a large, unsmiling lady in a tight black dress. She did not even
5 look up when I took my seat beside her. Her eyes were fixed on her plate and in a short time, she was busy eating. I tried to make conversation.
    'A new play is coming to "The Globe"
10 soon,' I said. 'Will you be seeing it?'
    'No,' she answered.
    'Will you be spending your holidays abroad this year?' I asked.
    'No,' she answered.
15   'Will you be staying in England?' I asked.
    'No,' she answered.
    In despair, I asked her whether she was enjoying her dinner.
    'Young man,' she answered, 'if you ate more and talked less, we would both
20 enjoy our dinner!'

a large, unsmiling lady

Fig. 6. (From *Practice and Progress* by L.G. Alexander (Longman))

Practice

What	am	I	painting
	are	you	doing
	is	he	cleaning
		she	cooking

I	am	painting a picture.
You	are	reading.
He	is	cleaning his car.
She		cooking a meal.

Make questions and answers for these pictures.

Example:

a

You write:

What's Brian Ford doing?
He's cleaning his car.

b

c

d

e

f

g

Look at this picture and then answer the questions.

1 Where are these people?
2 Where's Mr Brown sitting?
3 What's he reading?
4 What's he smoking?
5 What's Mrs Brown doing?
6 What's the little girl's name?
7 Where is she?
8 What's she doing?
9 Where's Tim sitting?
10 What's he doing?
11 Where's Jane?
12 What's she doing?

Fig. 7. (From *English Alive* by S. Nicholls, P. O'Shea and T. Yeadon (Edward Arnold))

Where visuals are both attractive as illustrations and integral to the course as teaching material, we have a bonus. Attractive presentation is certainly important, but it is of primary importance that visuals should be rooted in the teaching material rather than superimposed on it.

Videotaped material holds a good deal of potential for the language teacher as it allows presentation and practice of language in a very well contextualised manner. It has the advantage over 16mm film of being easier to handle and more versatile, and an obvious advantage over audiotape for language presentation is that the students have both visual and aural input and can make use of all the contextual clues provided by the gestures and facial expressions of the speaker and by the situation in which he is speaking. We are often guilty of underestimating the difficulty faced by learners when they are asked to listen to a disembodied voice coming out of a tape recorder. Using videotape certainly makes the students' task not only easier but also more realistic.

A very few courses, such as the *Follow Me* series produced by the BBC, make use of videotaped material as an integral part of the package. However, at the present time, the cost of making extensive use of videotaped courses is still prohibitive. But there will almost certainly be very important developments in this area in the not too distant future and videotape is a resource that language teachers should be thinking about very seriously in order to exploit fully its obvious potential.

1.2 Audio material

Recorded material is more and more frequently provided on cassette, although material on open-reel tapes is still widely available. Records (discs) are rarely offered nowadays and are not to be recommended as they lack a pause and review facility when played on standard turntables. What is recorded on tape is generally available in printed form as a tapescript, but it is necessary to listen to the actual tape to determine among other things the clarity of the recording and the kinds of voices used. Some tapes, mainly for listening comprehension, contain authentic material recorded on the spot, but by far the majority are recorded in a studio, often by professional actors and actresses. This may result in tapes which are in a sense 'overpronounced', where weak forms are stressed and the rhythm of speech is distorted. It is important to check that the spoken English on the tape is a fair representation of normal, colloquial, spoken English. Figure 8 opposte is an example of a tapescript.

1.3 Teachers' Books

A teacher's handbook is becoming a standard part of most courses now, although some still appear without one. Teachers' Books vary tremendously in the amount of assistance offered to the teacher. Some simply reproduce the student's book with a few additional notes for the teacher indicating the objective of each unit and suggesting ideas for one or two supplementary exercises. Others go into great detail and take the teacher step by step through every stage of every unit to the extent that every visual to be drawn on the board is given, with accompanying details of exactly what the teacher has to say at each given moment. The Teachers' Books for *Contact English* (Granger and Hicks, 1977) give very detailed instructions to the teacher along these lines and an extract from Teacher's Book 1 is reproduced in Figure 9 on page 54.

It must be said that it is better to err on the side of giving too much help rather

Five.
Doctor: I mean . . . well . . . er . . . something . . . something makes me nervous.
Patient: But what makes you nervous?

PRACTICE 4

Now you must ask both sorts of questions. Like this. Listen.

Doctor: Something seems strange.
Patient: What seems strange?
Doctor: When I look at you, I notice something.
Patient: What do you notice?
Now you do it. Ask the questions.
Doctor: Something seems strange.
Patient: What seems strange?
Doctor: I notice something.
Patient: What do you notice?
Doctor: When I look at you, something happens.
Patient: What happens?
Doctor: When I look at you . . . my heart . . . it . . . it does something.
Patient: What does it do?
Doctor: I mean . . . I want . . . I want to do something.
Patient: What do you want to do?
Doctor: But . . . er . . . something worries me.
Patient: What worries you?
Doctor: Your eyes . . . they . . . they do something to me.
Patient: What do they do to you?

Phase C *Further Practice*

PRACTICE 5

And now for something different. You're the doctor. You're talking to another doctor on the phone. Listen.
(Dialling)
Doctor: Doctor Barnes here.
Doctor: Hello, Doctor Barnes. This is Doctor Grant. I had one of your patients here yesterday.
Dr Barnes: Yes.
Dr Grant: And I want to tell you what he said . . . and what happened . . . and the questions he asked.

Dr Barnes: I see. Go on. That's the situation. You're the doctor. You're telling the other doctor what the patient said. Like this.
Yesterday the patient said this:
Patient: I'm very nervous.
So you say:
Dr Grant: He said he was very nervous.
Now you do it. Begin each sentence with "He said".
One.
Patient: I'm very nervous.
Dr Grant: He said he was very nervous.
Two.
Patient: I have headaches.
Dr Grant: He said he had headaches.
Three.
Patient: They worry me.
Dr Grant: He said they worried him.
Four.
Patient: I get them every day.
Dr Grant: He said he got them every day.
Five.
Patient: They're terrible.
Dr Grant: He said they were terrible.

PRACTICE 6

You're the doctor . . . you're still talking to the other doctor. But now you must tell the other doctor all the things you told the patient. Like this.

Yesterday you said:
Doctor: I know something about it.
So now you must say:
Doctor: I told him I knew something about it.
Now you do it. Begin each statement with "I told him".
One.
Doctor: I know something about it.
Doctor: I told him I knew something about it.
Two.
Doctor: It isn't serious.
Doctor: I told him it wasn't serious.
Three.
Doctor: Doctors know about this.
Doctor: I told him doctors knew about this.

Fig. 8. (From *Kernel Lessons Plus Tapescript*, R. O'Neill (Longman))

than too little, as a more experienced teacher can always disregard what he finds to be superfluous, whilst the detail in Teachers' Books such as those for *Contact English* can be of enormous help to the inexperienced or untrained teacher. A slight danger is that the experienced teacher might find it difficult to disregard the detailed instructions and as a consequence might feel that he is being forced into a mould that cramps his style. Certainly one would not wish to encourage a teacher in the belief that teaching consists largely, if not exclusively, of closely following minutely detailed instructions.

Some Teachers' Books compromise and provide detailed plans for teaching one or two units, and follow this up with more abbreviated notes for the rest of the units in the book. This schema would appear to satisfy the need of inexperienced teachers for a good deal of support, whilst encouraging them to become gradually more independent and decide for themselves how to use the material provided in the Students' Book.

9 | New Language | Long Present
he, she

Blackboard drawings

Introduction

Build up the first drawing, stopping
to ask questions as you draw:

| | What's this? | A head./A face. |

| | Is it a man or a woman? | A woman. |

| | What's this in her mouth? | A cigarette. |

| | What's she doing? | She's smoking. |
| | What's she smoking? | A cigarette. |

Presentation

Present the other drawings in the
same way, *e.g.*:

He's smoking a pipe.

Practice

Write a name under each picture—
let the class invent names if they
don't recognise the faces:

What's her name?   Matilda.

Write *Matilda*.

Then let students make statements
about the pictures:

Matilda's eating a banana.

George is drinking beer. *(etc.)*

Fig. 9. (From *Contact English* by C. Granger and T. Hicks (Heinemann))

Every teaching/learning situation is a unique combination of context and personality, and we should not expect to see materials used in exactly the same way, with dull uniformity, in all sorts of different situations. Ultimately it is up to the teacher to find his own way of teaching, one which suits the teacher and the class. With experience, the teacher's range of techniques will widen and his perception will sharpen. He will become less dependent on outside support, whether from colleagues or from books. So a Teachers' Book, whether brief or detailed, should be seen as a useful guide offering suggestions and advice. It should not be considered as a set of prescriptive instructions to be followed unquestioningly.

1.4 Vocabulary lists and indexes

Of particular use to the teacher are indexes and vocabulary lists, whether they occur in the Teacher's or in the Students' Book. An index of structures and/or an index of functions, preferably both, allows the teacher to locate quickly and easily any particular item for reference, or for remedial work. A vocabulary list should list all the vocabulary items used in the course up to the stage in question. For example, Book 3 of a four-stage course would list all the vocabulary used up to the end of stage 3 and additionally would indicate the unit in which each word was first introduced. With this information at his disposal the teacher who wishes to prepare some supplementary material of his own, to use a text from another source, or to write some test items can check quickly and easily whether a particular vocabulary item is already known to the students.

2 Materials for testing

The first question for consideration, clearly, is whether or not any materials for testing are included in the course. Very often they are not, in which case the teacher wishing to test the learners' performance will have to either write his own tests or use test materials from other published sources.

Where materials for testing are provided, we should consider their purpose, that is, what the tests are to be used for. In the context of a general course we might expect to find materials for **entry testing**, **progress testing**, and **achievement testing**. The purpose of the entry test is to determine whether the student's English is of a high enough standard for him to begin using the coursebook. (A beginners' book would not of course have an entry test!) An entry test may also have a diagnostic function in that it shows the teacher where a particular student's strengths and weaknesses lie and provides the teacher with a profile of the student's abilities.

Progress tests are given periodically during a course and are related directly to what has been taught in the preceding units, allowing the student to gauge his progress and the teacher to monitor the student's performance. Achievement tests also relate to the content of the course and would typically come at the end of each coursebook, corresponding to, say, a year's or a term's work.

Tests are valuable in that they tend to increase student motivation by providing a short-term goal and a means of checking one's own progress. They also provide the teacher with useful feedback which will help him to become more aware of the learning difficulties faced by the students. In this way the teacher can improve his own teaching performance.

The two main approaches to testing at present are, firstly, **discrete point** *testing* and, secondly, *communicative testing*. Discrete point testing concentrates on testing separately different language items and language skills (e.g. grammar, sound discrimination, listening with comprehension, writing) and by combining the results of a number of separate tests or test items builds up a picture of the student's level of English. This may be expressed as a single score or as a profile with a different score for different skills as shown in Figure 10 below.

STUDENTS' NAMES	LISTENING	SPEAKING	READING	WRITING	GRAMMATICAL ACCURACY
Françoise FAURE	6·3	5·4	6·1	4·8	5·9
Ayse ZOLTAN	7·1	4·5	5·4	3·6	4·1
Kees ALLES	8·2	8·8	7·8	6·9	8·7
Lotfi BEN BRAHIM	8·1	7·4	7·9	5·3	5·6

Fig 10. Results of discrete point tests expressed as student profiles

Discrete point testing can give a good idea of a student's performance in individual skills but it tends to neglect the fact that in communication we combine skills in a variety of ways, often with a severe constraint in real time. Communicative testing attempts to take account of this by testing a student's ability to perform in a communicative situation, using whatever combination of skills and abilities is necessary. The scoring will tend to be more subjective, as a global assessment is arrived at by making qualitative judgements according to a number of criteria such as *accuracy*, *flexibility* and *speed*.

Rather than breaking up the ability to use language into a large number of sub-skills, assessing them individually and adding up the scores, communicative testing assesses larger and more complex chunks of language, using *global tests* such as *cloze* and *dictation*, and relying on the subjective judgement of the tester aided by checklists of performance descriptions.

In general, we may ask two main things of tests which form part of a general course: they should relate well to the course itself and test what is taught in the course material, and they should reflect closely the learners' communicative needs by testing the sorts of abilities that the learners will need to use.

3 Other considerations

3.1 Teacher input

In general terms we may ask ourselves how much support the material provides the teacher with. Is a high degree of teacher input required, for example in supplementing the existing material, adapting it for presentation or working out the correct answers to difficult exercises, or is the material 'teacherproof', in other words so complete and self contained that it almost teaches itself, requiring the teacher simply to do what he is told? Another question is whether the material is easily taught by non-native speakers (surely the majority of EFL teachers fall into this category, although we sometimes tend to forget this fact) or whether the teacher would require a highly-developed native-speaker intuition to teach it. Some of the coursebooks which aim to teach communicative abilities, and in particular the appropriate use of stylistic variation, fall into the latter category because they rely on the teacher to recognise and often to produce English at different levels of formality in order to match the social context. Not only does the teacher have to perceive the social context correctly, he also has to select his language accordingly and make a number of very subtle and very difficult judgements. This is something that the native speaker can usually do well enough, but without very detailed support the non-native speaker may not be able to cope. Even across dialects of English the task is a difficult one, to the extent that British speakers of English often have difficulty in performing this kind of operation in American English, and vice-versa.

3.2 Equipment

The physical constraints imposed by a course may be considerable and in the absence of the necessary equipment some courses become virtually unusable. With inadequate equipment, the strain on the teacher can be immense, diverting his energies from the central task of teaching to fiddling around with machinery which he does not really understand. Some of the rather grandiose audio-visual courses of the 1960s are weak through their very sophistication. The fact that they need sophisticated equipment severely limits their application. There are, after all, many schools and colleges where even blacking out a room is a major problem. In this context we might ask ourselves if the material can still be used if certain items, such as filmstrips, are left out.

3.3 Subject matter

A very important consideration is the content, or subject matter, of a course. What do the dialogues contain? What do the reading passages actually tell us? What does the practice material actually relate to in the real world? If we are to get away from the claustrophobic situation of using language for its own sake, we need to see that the materials which we adopt make use of language in order to convey information, express opinions, etc. which are of genuine intrinsic interest to the learners. If through a reading passage the learners not only get exposure to English but also become interested in the subject matter, their motivation will be increased and they will see more purpose in learning the language. In this way the whole learning process will be enriched.

Unfortunately little general course material at present provides subject matter of genuine intrinsic interest, although it can be found in readers and in some listening materials, as well as in ESP courses. *Kernel Lessons Plus* (O'Neill, 1972) goes some way towards this goal in choosing a number of topics of general interest to adolescents and adults, and this approach surely must have contributed to the enormous popularity of the book. Many general courses today can be justly criticised for containing far too much fictional or fictitious material, lacking any literary merit, and not including enough interesting factual material for learners to get their teeth into.

3.4 Overall impression

Evaluating the overall composition of the material is a matter for personal judgement, taking into account the nature of the students and the type of teaching involved. The amount of visual material included in a coursebook, for example, can vary enormously from one course to another. What we should look for is a good balance between visual material and written text, so that each supports the other.

Summary

Most general courses include supplementary materials of various kinds and we should evaluate these individually and also as part of the whole package. We also need to know how much support is provided for the teacher and whether the material can be easily used by a non-native speaker. Some sophisticated courses require access to projection equipment and rooms with blackout facilities and this may be a limiting factor in many schools and colleges. Finally, we should consider the subject matter of the course to see whether it is of some intrinsic interest to the learners.

Exercises and activities

(a) Take a general course and see how many of the items listed in 6.1 in Chapter 10 it contains. Do you consider any of the omissions that you discovered to be serious? If YES, what problems would they cause, and how could the problems be overcome?

(b) Identify what testing materials there are which accompany your coursebook. What purposes could the testing material be used for? If there is no testing material, can you find any published tests which would be suitable? (See all the questions under 6.2 in Chapter 10.)

(c) If your course has a Teachers' Book, discuss how useful it is and the extent to which you use it. What would you like to see in it that isn't already there? Is there anything in the Teachers' Book that you consider unnecessary?

7 Motivation and the Learner

Motivation is arguably the most important single factor in success or failure at language learning. A well-motivated student badly taught will probably do better than a poorly-motivated student well taught. Motivation determines the student's level of attention during class, and the assiduity with which he does his homework and revises what he has been taught during the day. It certainly has a deep influence on the effectiveness of learning.

1 Psychological factors

Exactly what motivates students of English is difficult to determine and in any case it varies from one situation to another and from one person to another. Much motivation is external in that it does not stem from the quality of the teaching or the teaching materials at all but from social, economic and other factors.

1.1 Shorter-term objectives

There is evidence which shows that by setting realistic and attainable shorter-term objectives and by using materials which lead the pupil unambiguously towards those objectives, motivation can be considerably improved.

This claim is most obviously borne out in the developing area of ESP, where learners are taught to perform certain kinds of communicative acts in well-defined situations which are directly relevant to their education or employment and therefore to their personal advancement. Robinson (1980) refers to the 'purposefulness' of an ESP learning situation and Brumfit (1977) places ESP 'firmly within the general movement towards "communicative" teaching'.

Setting specific and relevant shorter-term objectives in the context of general language teaching is both feasible and beneficial. Buckby (1981) reports that the use of graded (short-term) objectives and tests in foreign language learning in British comprehensive (secondary) schools resulted in 'very significantly more positive attitudes... at all points of the aptitude scale' together with a significantly higher percentage of pupils opting for foreign language learning when it became optional (usually at the age of thirteen or fourteen) than the national average.

1.2 Appealing materials

Other points that we should look for in teaching materials are variety and pace, attractive appearance and feel, activities leading to personal involvement and 'self-investment' in the learning process, and activities with a competitive or problem-solving element in them.

A coursebook that is going to interest a learner should contain something that he wants to learn about or involve himself in, quite apart from the language itself. English should come over as a means of conveying messages of consequence and relevance and as a means through which one's experience is enriched and widened. It could well be presented as a 'window on the world'.

1.3 Whole-person approach

In the context of relevance to the learner, mention must be made of what has been called the whole-person approach to learning which derives from the **humanistic movement** in education. A very readable summary of humanistic values in education and their application to the language learning process can be found in Moskowitz (1978, chapters 1 and 2). Essentially it is concerned with developing and bringing into play all aspects of the learner's personality, and not just the cognitive or intellectual side. Consequently a good deal of emphasis is placed on the expression of feelings and attitudes on the part of the learner, together with a sense of sharing and supportiveness in the class as a whole.

Stevick (1980) applies humanistic values to materials evaluation in an informal way and suggests that 'whole-learner' materials should meet a number of criteria:

> (a) There should be something for the emotions as well as for the intellect.
>
> (b) The materials should provide occasions for the students to interact with one another.
>
> (c) The materials should allow students to draw on present realities as well as on their distant future goals.
>
> (d) The materials should provide for the students to make self-committing choices in the areas covered by (a)–(c) above.

The first criterion echoes the concern for the feelings and attitudes which is typical of humanistic education and one might add here that the primary concern should be less with sentimentality (and unfortunately some language-learning and language-using activities influenced by humanistic education do tend to give rise to sentimentality) than with volition. When given the opportunity to talk about their feelings and attitudes, students tend to *want* to communicate because they can convey things which are important to them and which are of immediate relevance to their present lives (Stevick's third criterion). In order for this to happen, interaction obviously must be encouraged, as has already been appreciated by mainstream TEFL thinking.

1.4 Realism

The concept of self-committing choices (Stevick's fourth criterion) means ensuring that the interaction in the classroom is as realistic as possible or, better, real in the full sense of the word, because the students are using English to say what they actually think and feel and so are using language realistically.

In this world of reality we spend a good deal of time talking about ourselves and about other people whom we know or know about. We do not normally discuss at length imaginary characters taken from a coursebook lacking literary merit (although it must be admitted that characters in television soap operas may come in for a fair amount of discussion because of the realism with which they are portrayed!). It follows that a major means of encouraging personal involvement and commitment is a fairly simple one: get the students to talk about themselves and other real people and to discuss real topics that are of immediate interest. It may seem obvious, but few coursebooks do it to any extent. Far commoner is the proliferation of cardboard characters, usually from bland middle-class families, whom the learners are supposed to talk about and at times impersonate. This, then, is a very important feature to look for in any general coursebook, and if it is lacking you should consider adapting the material to make it more directly relevant to the learners (see Chapter 9 for suggestions).

A further quotation from Stevick (1980, p.204) sums up some of these considerations:

> Whole learner materials...
>
> 1 would be written in a style that had some currency outside language textbooks
>
> 2 would convey some emotion
>
> 3 would be less bland in their content.

2 Social and cultural factors

2.1 Geographical setting

Many coursebooks have a readily definable cultural content which is evident in the subject matter of the course and the situations used to present and practice language items. Geographically, the setting is likely to be Britain or the United States, depending upon where the book is published and the market for which it is intended. Courses may also, however, have a non-English speaking country as their setting, and this is commonly the case in countries where English has the role of a second language. There is nothing strange or unreal in depicting two Indians or Nigerians using English to communicate with each other.

2.2 Age range and class

Other variables affecting the cultural content of a course include age, social class and occupation catered for. Because most learners of English tend to be secondary school pupils and young adults, the age range depicted and catered for in many courses is that of the late teens and twenties. Examples of this range from *Success with English* (Broughton, 1969) to the *Strategies* series (Abbs *et al*, 1975). The characters appearing in such courses tend to be middle class people living in or near London and having interesting jobs such as that of a journalist or an art-dealer.

2.3 Advantages of culture-specific coursebooks

The advantages of a specific cultural setting is that it provides a range of clearly identifiable situations for the presentation and subsequent practice of language items and so gives the course writer the opportunity to make his material meaningful through being contextualised. It also lends itself to the creation of recognisable characters who appear regularly throughout the course, giving a degree of continuity to the material and providing a sense of security for the student, who may well identify with one or more of them. Some of the characters may well feature in a serial story in the coursebook, providing the learner with added motivation to work through the course to the end.

2.4 Limitation of culture-specific coursebooks

A limitation of the culture-specific coursebook is that it will only be of relevance to students who understand the cultural background in which it is set. European learners, for example, would readily comprehend most cultural settings in Britain or the U.S.A., but the same cannot be said of learners in Iraq, Thailand, the Sudan or China, where cultural norms are vastly different. Indeed in these situations a strong portrayal of British life might well prove to be an impediment rather than a help to the learner. Unless the student is ultimately going to visit Britain or the U.S.A., the task of understanding and relating to the range of social situations portrayed in a culture-specific coursebook will be too great for any likely benefit accruing to justify it. The time would be better spent learning the language rather than the structuring of the social world in which the learner is never likely to find himself. The vast success of *First Things First* (Alexander, 1967) is no doubt in part due to its relative lack of culture specificity and the transparency of the situations in which language items are presented, making the book readily acceptable in almost any country in the world.

2.5 Teaching cultural background with the language

It follows from what I have written above that students who are intending to visit an English-speaking country for any length of time will need to be able to understand the social scene, and use English appropriately. A coursebook for this category of student should make clear and explicit links between social situations and language and should teach varieties of English which are appropriate to each particular situation.

There is a rather special situation in many European countries and also Japan, where, in the school system, the learning of English has as one of its main aims the gaining of insight into the 'civilisation' or 'life and institutions' of the English-speaking countries, again primarily Britain and the U.S.A. Here language learning is viewed in a broader context and is seen as a vehicle for understanding across national and cultural boundaries. Much of the content of coursebooks designed for such systems has the dual purpose of presenting language and conveying cultural information. The word **culture** here is being used in a general sense and does not solely refer to literature, music, painting, etc. but embraces all aspects of the pattern of life, the values, the problems and the achievements of a national grouping.

Points to consider when evaluating this kind of teaching material include the extent to which the overall picture given is representative of reality, whether the material is up-to-date and presents the contemporary scene rather than giving a historical perspective of life say twenty years ago, and whether there is any obvious bias for political or other reasons.

A danger in teaching language and cultural background together is the temptation to use at an early stage authentic (usually literary) texts which are far too advanced and lead the learner into a plodding process of literal translation. Even worse is the use of texts which no longer reflect current English usage (e.g. extracts from Dickens) and therefore cannot be said to provide the learners with a useful model of the language.

2.6 English as a second language

A learning situation very different from the culture-orientated approach outlined above is where English has the role of a **lingua franca** or a second language and is used for communication between groups of people who each have their own native language. People in many African and Asian countries use English in this way; Nigeria and India are good examples.

Course materials for use in this kind of situation will be very firmly rooted in the culture and traditions of the country where the teaching is to take place. English can be presented realistically and naturally in its role as a second language in use for a variety of purposes within the learners' own country. This state of affairs has the advantage that the learners can see the direct relevance of English to their daily lives and their future prospects, with all that this entails in terms of positive motivation.

2.7 Anthropological aspects of language

In conclusion it should be mentioned that any language-learning programme has a cultural content if we take culture in its anthropological sense. The vocabulary of English divides up reality in a particular way, and this is the way that English speakers see the world. English speakers have difficulty in using the French adjectives *grand* and *gros* because they do not correspond exactly in their range of meaning to the English adjectives *tall*, *big*, and *fat*. Similarly English distinguishes between honeydew melons and water melons, which are semantically related in that they are both thought of as being melons. However French, Turkish and some other languages spoken in the Mediterranean area have two completely different words for the two fruits (French: *melon* and *pastèque*; Turkish: *kavun* and *karpuz*) and they are commonly considered to be different fruits, not different kinds of the same fruit.

The learner of English not only has to learn the forms of English but also the conceptual system of English and this includes not only vocabulary but also, for example, the verb system and the way in which time relations are perceived. Some foreign learners have difficulty with the use of the present perfect in English because their conception of time relations is that of their own language, and they have to learn not only the form of the present perfect but also what it means and how it is used. They are learning an aspect of the culture of English-speakers because they are learning how an English-speaker perceives reality and categorises it.

Summary

Motivation is a major factor in language-learning success. We should look for material that has variety and pace, is of genuine interest to the learners and contains learning activities that will appeal to them. Activities which encourage personal involvement tend to increase motivation. The cultural standpoint of the course material is also important and should match as far as possible the objectives of the learner.

Exercises and activities

(a) Is the subject matter of your coursebook genuinely interesting? (See question 7.2 in Chapter 10.) If YES, list the topics which you and your students find most interesting. If NO, what topics do you think your students would be interested in?

  What sources can you think of for supplementary reading and/or listening material on interesting subjects?

(b) What is the cultural background of your coursebook? Do you feel that it is appropriate for your students? What suggestions could you make for improvements? (See 7.8 and 7.9 in Chapter 10.)

8 Overall Evaluation

Our consideration of criteria for materials evaluation has taken us through many areas of interest to the language teacher and has brought us into contact, however briefly, with several disciplines. I suggested earlier that the process of evaluation could not be a purely mechanical one and that professional judgement was involved at every stage. By examining teaching materials from a number of different perspectives and establishing explicit criteria for evaluation, we may hope to provide a basis for informed, professional judgement and decision making in this crucial area.

This judgement comes into play particularly in using the checklist in Chapter 10 and the individual user now has to make his own decisions. The points listed below (1 to 9) are suggestions which will help the user to arrive at an overall picture of a particular book if he is evaluating it in a general way without reference to one particular class or group of students, which is why numbers 6 and 7 ask which learning situations the book is suitable for and which situations it is unsuitable for.

1 Briefly state the objectives of the material.
2 To what extent is it successful in achieving these objectives?
3 Note particular strengths.
4 Note particular weaknesses.
5 Are there any notable omissions?
6 For what type of learning situations is the material suitable?
7 For what type of learning situations is the material unsuitable?
8 Comparisons with any other material evaluated.
9 General conclusion.

If you are evaluating material for a particular class in a particular situation you will probably have drawn up a list of the objectives which you wish to achieve with your class and you will then be in a position to match your teaching objectives against the potentialities of the material. Too great a discrepancy should send you searching for material elsewhere, but do not expect a perfect fit. Coursebooks are produced for a general market and for as large a market as possible. No coursebook is likely to be *ideally* suited to your class at its particular stage of development unless you are really lucky. So the aim should be to find the coursebook that most nearly meets your requirements and then you should be prepared to adapt the material to meet your special needs. Some ideas are given in the next chapter on how to adapt material in coursebooks so as to get a better match between materials and objectives.

Exercises and activities

(a) With reference to the coursebook you use, note down its good points and its bad points. On balance do you think that its good points outweigh its bad points or vice versa?
(b) Make a list of the features that are lacking in most present-day courses and that you would like to find in an ideal course to be published in the future. Discuss your ideas with others and build up a composite list. How many of the features in the composite list do you think could realistically be incorporated into a course?

9 Adaptation and Innovation: Making the Materials Meet Your Requirements

1 Inspiration and creativity

Except where a coursebook is prescribed by an education authority and so acts as a uniform syllabus for all schools, course materials for English should be seen as the teacher's servant and not his master. Writers of coursebooks may have greater experience, more extensive training or better resources to draw on than the average classroom teacher, but they do not have direct personal knowledge of each particular teacher's classes, school and country. The materials they produce should be seen as a basis on which to build, a raw material which can be fashioned by each individual teacher to meet his own needs.

We have looked so far in this book at many of the qualities that go into the formation of good teaching materials and we should now be in a position not only to evaluate and select materials in a sensible, systematic way but also to begin adapting material to suit individual needs and circumstances. It is rare that a piece of published material is wholly and completely suited to an individual teaching situation – there is nearly always scope for some adaptation and supplementation which adds a personal touch and makes the lesson more direct and relevant.

The checklist of evaluation criteria in Chapter 10 can be used to identify areas where adaptation is desirable; the course material then provides a basis and can often suggest possibilities for further development, serving as an inspiration to the teacher. Good teaching materials should indeed inspire both teacher and students. The teacher should be encouraged to move away from dependence on the material which he is using, towards a more creative and independent relationship in which imagination and an understanding of the students' difficulties and interests come into prominence.

The role of the coursebook can then be seen as that of an 'ideas bank', a source of practical examples of ideas for teaching particular topics and an inspiration which stimulates the teacher's own creative potential. The benefits of such a partnership between coursebook writer and teacher are considerable: the coursebook writer is no longer expected to do what he manifestly cannot do, which is to tailor the material to each individual class, and the teacher teaches in a more personal and creative fashion, with greater confidence and originality.

2 Some practical examples

Let us now look at some examples of how to adapt course material, basing our procedures on some principles of language teaching which have arisen in earlier chapters:

(a) Base language-learning procedures on models of actual communicative processes.

(b) Make learning activities relevant and purposeful.

(c) Meet your learners' needs, both external and psychological.

(d) Use models of real, authentic language.

For the first three of these examples I would like to take as a starting point a number of exercises from published sources, largely intended for practice of language items previously presented, and suggest how they might be adapted. This does not imply criticism of the exercises as they stand, indeed the fact that they provide the essential basis and inspiration is very much to their credit. Nor am I intending to give a series of prescriptive instructions for adaptations; this would be quite wrong as the scope is as wide as the experience and creativity of each individual teacher. The examples given here are themselves only modestly creative but will, it is hoped, serve as a model, however humble, of what can be achieved with a little thought and imagination.

A good starting point is to ask a few pertinent questions:

(i)   What does the exercise actually get the learner to do?

(ii) What do I want the learner to do?

(iii) How can I get the exercise to do what I want it to do for the learner?

2.1 Making dialogues communicative

The printed dialogue as a means of teaching the skills necessary to take part in a conversation is necessarily limited as it follows a development which is both pre-determined and external to the participants. Strictly speaking, two students reading a dialogue are not using language in a fashion which is representative of real language use because they are not speaking to any purpose beyond that of reading the dialogue. They are not developing their ability to produce the quick real-time responses which are an essential feature of fluency in a conversational context. A real-life conversation may develop along stereotyped lines, but in no case will it be written out beforehand and delivered to the participants in printed form!

A variant is the open dialogue where only one role is provided and the other is left blank for the student to say what he wants. This is perhaps more realistic but still is not an adequate model of oral/aural interaction. Let us consider what the student needs to do in the following extract, an open dialogue taken from *Strategies* (Abbs *et al*, 1975a, p.81):

Talk to Maggie about the things you used to do when you were younger.

Maggie: I used to go to school in a little village in Sussex. Where did you first go to school?

Student: ....

Maggie: Oh! What did you use to do in your free time? Anything interesting?

Student: ....

Maggie: Mmm. Did you? I used to go riding. Did you?

Student ....

Maggie:	Really? And I used to collect wild flowers. Did you use to collect anything when you were young?
Student:	....
Maggie:	How interesting! Do you still collect anything?
Student:	....

The student, it will be seen, is really engaged in answering a series of questions. He responds to what Maggie asks, but is given no opportunity of initiating anything, or rather if he does initiate anything, the open dialogue breaks down. Suppose that the student's third response in the dialogue is: 'No, but we spent a lot of time swimming. How about you? Do you like swimming?' This is perfectly natural and in fact more natural than simply answering a series of questions, but it would not fit into the dialogue and the student is required to restrict himself, like a witness in court, to answering the question.

In order therefore for the open dialogue to work, the student has to formulate his answer so that it will fit what Maggie says next. In other words he has to read what Maggie will say in response to the student's utterance and formulate the utterance accordingly. Such a process is impossible in real conversation which proceeds sequentially in real time. I do not wait to hear what the response is to my utterance and then decide to say something that fits the response. If the student's second response in the open dialogue were, 'I never really had any free time', the dialogue would again break down. Similarly, if the fourth response were 'I never could stand collecting things'.

In the Teacher's Book for *Strategies* the authors state that: 'the students should be encouraged to give answers according to their own experience' and teachers are told to 'insist that the students' answers are true'. In certain circumstances, however, as we have seen, the fact of the student drawing on his own experience and giving true answers *could* cause the activity to break down. This is not to suggest that open dialogues are of no value, but simply to point out that we should ask ourselves what an exercise *actually* gets the learner to do.

The following open dialogue taken from *Kernel One* (O'Neill, 1978, p.70) allows the student (referred to as 'you') to initiate the conversation, but again the initiation cannot take place until the student has read and understood the answer, and of course in reality if he knows the answer he no longer needs to ask the question.

You are asking Frank questions	
1 YOU:	....
FRANK:	Me? In Manchester.
2 YOU:	...., too?
FRANK:	Yes, they were.
3 YOU:	....?
FRANK:	At school? Well, I wasn't very good and I wasn't very bad, either.

To suggest that such exercises are of no value because they are not wholly realistic is of course nonsense. They have an important role to play in providing a framework for controlled language practice. However we must take our students beyond this point if we are to prepare them to communicate. We must progressively reduce the amount of control and give the student more opportunity to respond in real time.

To this end we can adapt certain coursebook dialogues and turn them into pair-work exercises based on cue cards. Here each student is given a card which gives instructions for performing a sequence of communicative acts which will interlock with a corresponding sequence indicated on the partner's card. In this way each student, being unable to anticipate the partner's next response, must react in real time and so will develop the ability to respond quickly, something which conventional dialogue work will not equip them to do.

A pair of cards developed from the open dialogue shown on page 67 would look like this:

Card A   You are talking to someone that you don't know very well. Begin the conversation with a question.

1 Ask him where he was born.

2 Ask if his parents were born there too.

3 Ask if he was good at school.

4 Respond (tell the truth!).

Card B   Someone you don't know very well asks you some questions.

1 Answer the question.

2 Answer the question.

3 Answer the question. Ask if he is a student or if he has a job.

It can be seen that, with this method, the turn-taking can be made more natural with a more even distribution of question and answer, and a greater opportunity for telling the truth without the activity breaking down. One could of course devise sequences that are not made up of question and answer routines at all, but are based on agreement and disagreement, for example. An interesting procedure is to listen to a number of short informal conversations in, say, the staff room, or on a bus, or in a shop and note them down briefly, or if possible record them. Then, simplifying and abbreviating as necessary, turn them into sets of cue cards for use with your students.

2.2 Making learning activities relevant and purposeful

We use language for a wide variety of purposes, usually social, so it is not unnatural that we should wish our language-learning activities to be purposeful in a social context, and consequently relevant to our learners as individuals. One way of doing this is to personalise classroom activities so that students are learning about each other, expressing their own ideas and feelings and generally communicating about things that matter.

Suppose that we wish to teach the difference in *use* between the simple past and the present perfect in English (we can assume that the form of these two tenses is already known). A good example of a non-personalised exercise to practice this point is provided in *A Practical English Grammar, Exercises 1* (Thomson and Martinet, 1961) which is still widely used. In exercise 15 on p.27 we find the instructions:

> Put the verbs in brackets into the present perfect or the simple past tense and fill the spaces by repeating the auxiliary used in the question.

followed by some examples and then the exercise proper:

> 1 Have you wound the clock?   (a) Yes, I . . .
>   (b) Yes, I (wind) it on Monday
> 2 Have you ever eaten snails? (a) No, I . . .
>   (b) Yes, I (eat) some at Tom's party last week
> 3 Has she fed the dog?   (a) Yes, I think she . . .
>   (b) Yes, she (feed) him before lunch

Although this is useful practice of language form, and includes first and second persons as well as the third person, no one is actually saying anything which is true (except coincidentally) or which serves any purpose, beyond the immediate purpose of practising language.

To teach the use of these tenses it would be more effective and meaningful to draw on the students' own experiences and allow them to share these experiences, whilst essentially following the same model as in the book of exercises. Ask the class 'Who's visited New York?' If no one has, elicit where New York is and why no one in class has visited it (too far, too expensive to travel there, too dangerous, etc.) and then pass on to another town or country until you find somewhere which has been visited by one or two students only. The sequence continues:

> Teacher Have you visited New York, Frank?
> Student Yes, I have.
> Teacher How many times have you visited New York?
> Student Once.
> Teacher When did you go there?
> Student I went there in 1978.

The teacher is in the process of establishing through the context of reality that the same action, in this case visiting New York (the same because the student only went there once), can be represented by two different verb forms or tenses, depending not upon objective differences between two actions but upon the speaker's subjective considerations, upon where he is focusing his attention. In this example, of course, the contrast is between an action seen in the context of the past (past simple) and an action viewed in terms of its relevance to the present (present perfect). The fact that the action is real and is referred to in a communicative way reinforces the teaching point more directly than would otherwise be the case.

This particular activity could be developed in a variety of ways. For example, students divide into small groups and build up a list of countries they have visited, films they have seen, books they have read, etc. and when. At the end of the activity the findings of the different groups are put up on the board and compared.

Many imaginative exercises in coursebooks can be personalised relatively easily and with a minimum of effort on the part of the teacher. There is a useful exercise for practising *ought to* in *Strategies* (Abbs *et al*, 1975a, p.121). A number of advertisements are presented for a variety of activities such as taking a secretarial course, visiting the National Theatre, and going to a concert, together with the model sentence:

I ought to learn a foreign language but I haven't got the energy.

The students make further sentences based on the model and using the advertisements as cues, e.g.

I ought to go to a concert but I haven't got the energy.
I ought to look for a new flat but I haven't got the time.

In the personalised adaptation of the exercise, each student is asked to think of and note down two or three activities which have enriched his life in the past year or so, and, if possible, say what the results have been. Then in pairs or small groups, the students give each other advice such as:

You (really) ought to go swimming once a week. I swim regularly and it makes me healthy.

The response to this can be:

Yes, I ought to, and I will or
I ought to, but I haven't got the time/energy.

Disagreement can be expressed by:

I ought to? No, I don't think so.

As an alternative, or additional exercise, students can talk about any minor problems that they have and seek advice from their fellow students who can respond using the structure:

You ought to see a doctor/change your job, etc.

Such exchanges often become humorous, and, so long as the situation does not get out of control, it is a good development, indicating that the students' interests and emotions are fully engaged and that English is being used to effect.

2.3 Meeting your learners' needs, both external and psychological

Students, particularly more sophisticated adults and teenagers, need to feel that the material from which they are learning has relevance to the real world and at the same time relates positively to aspects of their inner make-up such as age, level of education, social attitudes, intellectual ability, and level of emotional maturity.

It is very common, when searching through coursebooks for suitable materials, to come across exercises which superficially may appear quite unsuitable for a particular class but which on closer scrutiny are seen to be excellent in conception and only inappropriate to a particular teaching situation because of their subject matter or style.

A positive approach to published materials is to look below the surface and perceive the way in which the exercise works. If the basic idea is good, it can probably be used with different subject matter, at a different level or with language which is different stylistically.

Here is an exercise in writing taken from *Guided Composition Exercises* (Spencer, 1967), which is a veritable mine of ideas and techniques for teaching writing skills at the level of the sentence and the paragraph. The aim of the exercise is to select a number of verbs from a range of alternatives partly on the basis of style, (e.g. *climbed* not *ascended* the wall), partly according to what are acceptable collocations (e.g. *picked* but not *plucked* the apples) and partly by recognising what is normal or logical in behaviour (e.g. he *ran* home, he did not *march*, because that would not be normal behaviour and he did not *limp* because we know that he did not hurt himself). This exercise then teaches (and tests) the ability of the learner to use appropriate lexis, selected according to one of a number of possible criteria.

Write the following passage out again, adding, in the spaces indicated by numbers, one verb from the lists with the corresponding numbers given below the passage. In each group of three verbs one is more appropriate in the context than the other two.

The boy (1) the wall (2) the apples. He (3) half-a-dozen and (4) them in his pockets. As he was (5) down again he slipped and (6). The fruit in his pockets was squashed. He did not (7) himself, but he could not (8) the apples either. He (9) home and (10) his coat pockets.

(1) climbed, leapt, ascended
(2) discover, reach, inspect
(3) plucked, seized, picked
(4) hid, put, laid
(5) jumping, slipping, falling
(6) slid, collapsed, fell
(7) wound, hurt, cut
(8) eat, taste, use
(9) marched, limped, ran
(10) cleaned, washed, changed

Some of the choices that have to be made are fairly sophisticated and demand considerable insight into the way English lexis is used. In comparison, the subject matter of the exercise is relatively trivial and inconsequential. Within the context of the exercise, what purpose is there in making the necessary choices beyond the rather artificial one of using language in order to use language?

The underlying idea however is a good one and can be used to good effect in a richer and more promising context. Suppose that the teacher aims to develop sensitivity to appropriateness of lexis in specific linguistic contexts with an upper-intermediate class. The teacher takes a newspaper article on something of topical and direct interest to the students and identifies a number of words in the article to explore further in class. The teacher delates those words from the article and presents them together with less appropriate alternatives in a similar manner to Spencer's in the exercise above. If the teacher wishes to emphasise style then the alternatives will be stylistically less appropriate than the original; if he wishes to stress collocation, then the alternatives will be collocationally unacceptable even though their meaning makes sense; and so on.

The exercise is presented to the learners working in groups of three or four in the following terms: 'Imagine that you are a group of sub-editors of a newspaper and that an article has been submitted by a reporter who is very indecisive. He sometimes just can't make up his mind what word to use. Discuss the alternatives that he has put forward in your groups and agree on the best word to use in each case, if possible saying why.'

Each group works on the same text and after sufficient time has been allowed, the decisions of each group are compared and an acceptable version of the text is built up before the whole class. With advanced classes the choices can be far less clear-cut and a number of possibilities can emerge, each with its own justification.

2.4 Using real, authentic language

Clearly all teaching material, particularly at the earlier stages of learning, cannot and should not be composed of authentic language. It is, however, beneficial to the learner's confidence and motivation, and therefore to his overall learning performance, to be able to cope with a limited amount of authentic language. At the earlier stages this might be best done through reading, as the learner has the opportunity when reading of re-reading the text as many times as he wishes and does not have to operate within strict time constraints. However, carefully selected listening material can also be used successfully, particularly if taped material can be used in a language laboratory or listening centre so that each student can progress at his own speed.

Many recent coursebooks incorporate elements of authentic language such as timetables, menus, notices, and advertisements. These are exponents of English which can be processed fairly immediately and from which factual information can be extracted. It is not essential for the student to understand everything in order to identify and assimilate the essential information.

The following is an example of how an authentic text (in this case a London Transport information leaflet) can be used for reading for information and can form the basis of a communicative activity which requires integration of language skills.

The London Transport Project

Take a copy of London Transport's Official Tourist Information leaflet, which is issued free at London Transport Travel Information Centres and, outside Britain, is available from most British Tourist Authority offices. Cut it into three parts so that each part contains more or less an equal amount of information. For example one part can consist of information on buses, the second part information on the underground and the third part information on special tickets and services for tourists.

Mount each part on a separate card. Now prepare *one* worksheet with questions requiring the extraction of information from the whole leaflet. There should be about four questions which can be answered from each of the three cards, giving about twelve questions in all.

Phase One. Divide the class into three small groups of three to six students in each group. (If you class is large, you can run the activity in duplicate or triplicate – you simply need more than one set of materials.) Each group has one card and has to answer as many questions on the worksheet as it can, using the information on its card. They write the answers on the worksheet.

Phase Two. The groups now exchange information orally, usually in question-and-answer sequences, until each group can write down the answers to all the questions on the worksheet. The task is then completed.

The skills and abilities practised by this activity include: reading and extracting information; writing down information in note form; making and understanding requests for information in the spoken medium; providing orally information that has been requested, using written notes as a source; querying requests; confirming information that has been queried. The model, which is based upon the concepts of information gap and willingness to communicate, is representative of authentic interaction even though the basis of the activity is contrived, and it simulates well some of the strategies and skills necessary for effective and purposeful use of language. (See Cunningsworth, 1979 for a more detailed description of this procedure.)

Exercises and activities

(a) Take a dialogue from a coursebook familiar to you and analyse what the students actually do when practising with it. Adapt the dialogue as necessary and turn it into a pair of cue cards along the lines described on page 68. What do you think are the advantages and disadvantages of cue cards compared with coursebook dialogues?

(b) Choose an exercise for teaching pronunciation from a coursebook and adapt it to make it more interesting and more meaningful.

(c) Take a piece of authentic language (written or spoken) and discuss how you could exploit it for teaching purposes.

10 Checklist of Evaluation Criteria

The criteria for evaluation discussed in Chapters 2–8 are summarized here in the form of a checklist of questions to ask about EFL teaching materials. The questions are numbered chapter by chapter.

Some of the points can be checked off either in polar terms (i.e. yes or no) or, where we are talking about *more* or *less* of something, on a gradation from 1 to 5. A straight yes or no answer is required to the questions such as 6.2 'Are there any materials for testing?' However, in many cases such a simple choice would only very inadequately reflect the nature of the course material and there would be a consequent danger of oversimplification. It is, for example, rare for material to assume a wholly inductive or deductive learning process on the part of the learner (for comparison of inductive and deductive learning, see p. 32) and some form of compromise is usually achieved whereby the writer has used both approaches and we, as users, need to know approximately the proportion of one to the other. In this case it would be useful if the reader thought in terms of the relative weighting given to each approach by the materials writer and indicated this descriptively as, for example, in question 4.1.2.

Is the language learning process assumed to be essentially
- inductive
- deductive
- a combination of both?

where the answer may be 'essentially inductive but significant elements of deductive learning'. Alternatively the reader could use a five point scale, and indicate the relative weightings on it:

Inductive	1	2	3 x 4	5
Deductive	1 x 2	3	4	5

Other questions on the checklist cannot be answered in quantitive terms but require an evaluative or descriptive comment. For example,

> 4.3 Comment on the presentation and practice of new lexis (vocabulary). How is new lexis presented (e.g. in word lists, with visuals, in a text)? How is the meaning of new lexis taught (e.g. through context, through explanation, by translation)?

The checklist is intended as an instrument, or a useful tool, for evaluating teaching material. It is not an automatic procedure such as an algorithm that will guide the user progressively towards the 'right' answer. The reason for this is that there are too many variables involved, and many of the variables depend upon the professional judgement of the person carrying out the evaluation exercise. Professional judgement, founded on understanding of the rationale of language teaching and learning and backed up by practical experience, lies at the base of the evaluation procedure.

Chapter 2 Language content

2.1 What apects of the language system are taught? To what extent is the material based upon or organised around the teaching of:

(a) language form (see 2.2)

(b) language function

(c) patterns of communicative interactlon?

2.2 Which aspects of language form are taught?

(a) phonology (production of individual sounds, stress, rhythm, intonation)

(b) grammar   (i) morphology
              (ii) syntax

(c) vocabulary (lexis)

(d) discourse (sequence of sentences forming a unified whole)

2.3 What explicit reference is there to appropriateness (the matching of language to its social context and function)? How systematically is it taught? How fully (comprehensively) is it taught?

2.4 What kind of English is taught?
(a) dialect   (i) class
                (ii) geographic
(b) style   (i)   formal
                (ii) neutral
                (iii) informal

(c) occupational register
(d) medium   (i) written
                (ii) spoken

2.5 What language skills are taught?
(a) receptive   (i) written (reading)
                (ii) spoken (listening)

(b) productive (i) written (writing)
                (ii) spoken (speaking)

(c) integration of skills
    e.g. note taking, dictation, reading aloud, participating in conversation

(d) translation (i) into English
                (ii) from English

Chapter 3 Selection and grading of language items

3.1   Does the material follow
          (a) a structural syllabus

          (b) a functional syllabus?

3.2   Is the selection and sequence of the language to be taught based on:
          (a) an attempt to identify probable student need
              (*student-centred approach*)

(b) the internal structure of the language (*subject-centred approach*)?

3.3 Grading and recycling

3.3.1 Is the grading of the language content
(a) steep

(b) average

(c) shallow?

3.3.2 Is the progression
(a) linear

(b) cyclical?

3.3.3 Is there adequate recycling of
(a) grammar items

(b) lexis (vocabulary)?

Chapter 4 Presentation and practice of new language items

4.1.1 What are the underlying characteristics of the approach to language teaching?
(a) influence of behaviourist learning theory

(b) influence of the cognitive view

(c) a combination of both

(d) other influences (e.g. group dynamics, humanistic education)

4.1.2 Is the language learning process assumed to be essentially
(a) inductive

(b) deductive

(c) a combination of both?

4.2 Presentation and practice of grammar items

4.2.1 Comment on the presentation of new structures (grammar items). How are new structures presented? To what extent is the presentation:
(a) related to what has been previously learned

(b) meaningful (in context)

(c) systematic

(d) representative of the underlying grammar rule

(e) appropriate to the given context

(f) relevant to learners' needs and interests?

4.2.2 Comment on practice activities for new structures. Are they
(a) adequate in number

(b) varied

(c) meaningful

    (d) appropriate to the given context

    (e) relevant to learners' needs and interests

    (f) sufficiently controlled?

4.3 Comment on the presentation and practice of new lexis (vocabulary).
    (a) How is new lexis presented (e.g. in word lists, with visuals, in a text)?

    (b) How is the meaning of new lexis taught (e.g. through context, through explanation, by translation, through the use of semantic relations e.g. synonymy, hyponymy)?

    (c) Is new lexis recycled adequately?

    (d) What is the amount of new lexis taught in each unit, text etc.? (This can be expressed as a percentage of new lexis in relation to familiar lexis. See page 40.)

4.4 Is there any systematic attempt to teach the phonological (sound) system? If so, comment on content and method of teaching under the following headings:
    (a) Recognition of individual sounds (phonemes)

    (b) Production of individual sounds (phonemes)

    (c) Recognition and understanding of stress patterns and intonation contours

    (d) Production (in appropriate contexts) of stress patterns and intonation contours

Chapter 5 Developing language skills and communicative abilities

5.1 Free production of speech

5.1.1 What activities are there for free production of spoken English?

5.1.2 What is the relative proportion of time devoted to presentation of new language items, to practice of these items, and to free production activities?

5.2 Materials for reading, listening and writing

5.2.1 Comment on the extent and nature of reading texts and accompanying exercises.

5.2.2 Comment on the extent and nature of listening materials and accompanying exercises.

5.2.3 Comment on the extent and nature of writing exercises.

5.3 Integrated skills and communicative abilities

5.3.1 What activities are there for integrating language skills?

5.3.2 What activities are there for communicative interactions and the teaching of communication strategies?
Are they representative of and modelled on the processes that take place in real language use?

5.3.3 Are there any exercises that implicitly or explicitly teach how to combine functional units of language to create discourse and how to recognise the structure of discourse?

Chapter 6 Supporting materials

6.1 Does the course material include the following? If so evaluate usefulness in each case.
(a) visual material

(b) recorded material

(c) examples of authentic language

(d) a teacher's book

(e) an index of grammar items, functions etc.

(f) a vocabulary list (preferably indicating in which unit each word is first used)

6.2 Are there any materials for testing?

6.2.1 If so, are there materials for
(a) entry testing (diagnostic testing)

(b) progress testing

(c) achievement testing?

Are there any suggestions for informal continuous assessment?

6.2.2 Are the tests
(a) discrete item tests

(b) communicative tests

(c) a combination of both?

6.2.3 Do the tests relate well to
(a) the learners' communicative needs

(b) what is taught by the course material?

6.3 Other considerations

6.3.1 Evaluate the degree of support for the teacher and the amount and quality of guidance provided.
(a) Does the material require a high degree of teacher input?

(b) Is the material almost self-sufficient (teacherproof)?

(c) Is it suitable for a teacher who is not a native speaker?

(d) Does it require the teacher to have a native speaker intuition?

6.3.2 Does the material impose any specific physical restraints (e.g. material only usable in darkened room with projection facilities; material requiring regular use of a language laboratory)?

6.3.3 Does the subject matter contained in the course material have any intrinsic interest in its own right (or is it transparently a pretext for language work)?

6.3.4 Evaluate the overall composition of the material (i.e. the relationship of the parts to the whole).

Chapter 7 Motivation and the learner

7.1 Does the material have variety and pace?

7.2 Is the subject matter of reading texts, listening passages, etc. likely to be of genuine interest to the learners, taking into account their age, social background and cultural background, their learning objectives and the composition of the class?

7.3 Are the learning activities in the course material likely to appeal to the learners (taking into account the variables mentioned in 7.2 above)?

7.4 Does the material have an attractive appearance (visuals, layout, typography etc.)?

7.5 Do the activities in the material encourage the personal involvement of the learners in the learning process (e.g. by talking about themselves or finding out about each other)?

7.6 How much responsibility for the learning process is to be assumed by the learners themselves, individually or collectively?

7.7 Is there a competitive or problem-solving element in the learning activities?

7.8 Does the material have a specific cultural setting (e.g. young, trendy, middle-class London) or is it non culture-specific?

7.9 If material is culture-specific, will this be acceptable to the learners?

7.10 Does the material include aspects of British and/or American culture so that language learning is seen as a vehicle for cultural understanding?

7.11 Is the cultural context included only to provide a setting for the content of the material (i.e. is cultural context subordinated to language learning)?

7.12 Does the cultural context of the material guide the learners in perceiving and categorising the social situation they may find themselves in, with a view to helping them to match their language to the situation (i.e. to use English appropriately)?

Chapter 8 Conclusions and overall evaluation

8.1 Briefly state the objectives of the material.

8.2 To what extent is it successful in achieving these objectives?

8.3 Note particular strengths.

8.4 Note particular weaknesses.

8.5 Are there any notable omissions?

8.6 For what type of learning situations is the material suitable?

8.7 For what type of learning situations is the material unsuitable?

8.8 Comparisons with any other material evaluated.

8.9 General conclusion.

A Glossary of Basic EFL Terms
by Brian Tomlinson

This glossary is written for people who have little training or experience in teaching English as a foreign language but who want an understanding of the basic terminology of this field in order to help them in their work or in their studies.

Each term is defined briefly and in some cases reference is then made to specific short sections of books which could help the reader to gain a fuller understanding of the uses of the term. Details of books referred to are given in the bibliography on page 00.

Abbreviations
cf. = compare
∴ = therefore
X = contains an error

Achievement tests
Language tests which test what the learner has been taught.

cf. **Attainment tests**

Acquisition

The process of picking up a language without formal instruction and without a sustained conscious effort to learn the language. Acquisition usually occurs as a result of highly motivated exposure to the language in use plus the need and opportunity to communicate in the language. Children acquire their first language in this way and are capable of picking up any language anywhere without tuition. Adults are capable of acquiring the ability to communicate in a foreign language in this informal way too but most seem to need some conscious, formal learning as well in order to achieve accuracy.

See Krashen (1981, pp.1–3)
See **Learning**

Analytical
An analytical approach is one which gets the learners first of all to respond to and use chunks of language which include a variety of structures etc. and then to focus on those structures etc. with which they have problems.

cf. **Synthetic**

Anaphoric reference

The use of a word or phrase to refer back to a word or group of words previously mentioned. In the following examples, the words with anaphoric reference are in italics:

My mother is Hungarian but *she* speaks fluent English.
Mary knows the beer is in the fridge because *she* put *it* there.

Appropriacy
Language use is only really correct if the utterances are appropriate to the situations in which they are used. The roles and status of the language users, the roles and relationships of any other participants, the topic and the setting are some of the situational factors that determine appropriacy of language use. Thus 'That's rubbish', could be appropriate as a matter of disagreement in a discussion in a pub between friends about a football match, but would be inappropriate if used by someone being interviewed by the manager of a company he has applied to join.

Attainment tests
Language tests which seek to discover information about the language abilities of the learner(s). Unlike achievement tests they are not restricted to testing what learners have been taught.

Audio aids
Aids such as radios, record players, tape recorders and language laboratories which help the learners by exposing them to the spoken language.

Audio-lingual approach
An approach to language teaching based on listening and then speaking. It relies heavily on oral imitation, memorization and drills designed to produce correct language habits.

See Behaviourist theories

Audio-visual aids
Aids such as televisions, films and video equipment which allow the learners to see a situation as well as listen to the language used in it.

Aural comprehension
Activities which involve the learners listening to and responding to spoken language.

Authentic materials
Materials such as newspaper articles, brochures, train tickets, letters, advertisements, recordings of the news, airport announcements, etc. which were originally used in real situations and were not designed for use in language teaching. Such materials are used in the classroom to expose the learners to language in real use.

Authentic tasks
Responses to written or spoken material which would be natural to real participants in a real situation. For example, learners in a classroom who read a text telling them what is on at the theatres in a city and then decide which theatre to go to.

Auxiliary verbs
Verbs which help the main verb in an utterance. They either perform a function for the main verb (as in the examples under (a)) or they add to the meaning of the main verb (as in the examples under (b)).

    (a) (i)   He *has* gone (i.e. tense formation)
          (ii) *Did* you win? (i.e. question formation)
          (iii) She is coming, *isn't* she? (i.e. question-tag formation)
          (iv) Do you love me?
               Of course I *do*. (representing the main verb)
    (b) (i)   You *should* work harder.
          (ii) I *must* go now.
          (iii) She *ought* to be ready.

The verbs in italics in (b) are usually referred to as modal verbs.

See Modal verbs

Backwash effect
The effect that the nature of the final examination has on the teaching and learning during a course. An examination which focuses on tests of grammatical knowledge is likely to lead to the teaching and learning of grammatical knowledge in courses preparing candidates for the examination, whereas a communicative examination is likely to encourage communicative approaches and activities in the classroom.

Behaviourist theories
Theories based on the assumption that language learning is a process of habit formation relying on correct imitation and frequent repetition.

cf. Cognitive approaches

Bilingual
A person able to speak a second language as well as if it was his or her first language, or a person with two first languages.

Cf. Multilingual
See First language Second language

Cloze test
A test of language proficiency in which the learner has to fill in blanks in a continuous passage. There are many variations on the cloze test but the basic type involves the setter selecting a passage and then deleting every nth word. Most EFL cloze tests require learners to complete a passage from which every seventh or eighth word has been deleted but an advanced level test might be based on a deletion rate of five or six.

See Heaton (1975, pp. 122–124)

Cognitive approaches
Approaches to language teaching which involve the learners thinking about the language and working out rules from examples or instances.

See Examples Instances

Coherence
The linking together of consecutive utterances in accordance with the function of the utterances. Thus an invitation followed by an acceptance or a generalisation followed by an example would be coherent whereas a factual enquiry followed by an anecdote would not be coherent.

     A Would you like to come to dinner tomorrow?
     B I'd love to. Thanks.
(coherent)
     A Could you tell me which platform the London train leaves from, please?
     B I went to London last week to see my daughter Alice. She lives in Chelsea, you know.
(not coherent)

See Widdowson (1978, pp. 27–29, pp. 38–44)

Cohesion
The logical linking of consecutive or related utterances.
Example (1)
     My *father* is always tired in the evenings. *He* goes to work at six in the morning *and* doesn't get home till seven.
Example (2)
     I agree that *he's* a very experienced player. *He's* played for Yugoslavia many times and *he's* played in a European Cup Final. *However*, I don't think *the club* should pay all *that money* for *him*.
See Widdowson (1978, pp. 24–27 and pp. 32–38)

Collocation
Words which are frequently used together are said to be collocates. Thus 'pillow', 'bed', 'sleep', and 'sheet' are collocates but 'cushion' and 'bed' are not; 'pick' and 'flowers' are collocates but 'pick' and 'grass' are not.

Communication gap
The disparity in knowledge and experience that exists between people involved in

communication with each other. The wife who asks her husband , 'Who won?', the doctor who asks his patient, 'How do you feel today?' and the policeman who directs a motorist to, 'Turn right at the cinema', are doing so because of a 'communication gap'.

Much of the interaction between the teacher and the learners in the classroom is extremely artificial because there is no 'communication gap' between the participants. For example:

Teacher   I'm drawing on the board. What am I doing?
Learners You're drawing on the board.
Teacher   Am I writing on the floor?
Learners No, you're not writing on the floor.

In order to give a group of learners opportunities to use language in a meaningful way, it is important to make sure that there are communication gaps in the situations in which the learners are asked to perform (e.g. the learners do not know the answers to questions a situation encourages them to ask.)
Note Some books use the term 'information gap' instead of 'communication gap'.

Communicative activities
Activities designed to get learners to use the language for communication rather than for language practice. The main aims of these activities are to help the learners to gain confidence, to become more fluent and to acquire language through exposure and use. They are not designed to provide practice and correction of specific language Items.

See **Acquisition Fluency Use**

Communicative approaches
Approaches to teaching EFL which stress the importance of learning through using the language and which give the learners frequent opportunities to interact with each other and with the teacher in 'natural' situations.

See **Acquisition Interaction Use**

Communicative competence
A measure of a learner's ability to achieve successful communication in the language he is learning.

Communicative effect
Whenever we use language we do so to achieve a purpose. The communicative effect of an utterance is a measure of the extent to which the purpose of the utterance is achieved.
For example:
A Why don't you use sand?
B That's a good idea. I think I will.
A has achieved his purpose in getting a suggestion accepted.

Communicative tests
Tests designed to discover the learners' abilities to communicate in English rather than to test their knowledge of particular language items or aspects of the language.

cf. **Discrete point tests**

Community language learning
A method of language learning which relies upon the learners to provide their own syllabus. The learners form a circle with their chairs and start a conversation. The teacher (referred to as a 'knower' or 'resource person') stays outside the circle and waits for a learner to ask for help. When this happens he whispers an English trans-lation or a corrected English version for the learner to then use in the conversation. The group conversation is recorded and transcribed and is later analysed by the

learners and the teacher. This analysis then provides the basis for the teaching of particular language points.

See Stevick (1976, pp. 125–133)
See **Learner centred approaches**

Competence
A confusing term because it is used with different meanings by different writers.

It was used to refer to an idealised grammar which was supposed to underlie the ideal user's language performance but is nowadays mainly used to refer to knowledge about a language as opposed to the ability to use the language in real situations.

See Communicative competence

Connotation
The associations which a word or group of words has for a particular language user or community of language users. Thus 'rebel' and 'freedom fighter' could be used by two different speakers to refer to the same person. The two phrases have the same referent but different connotations. In the same way 'conservative' might have the same referent but different connotations for different people.

cf. **Denotation**
See Ellis and Tomlinson (1980, 'Implied Meaning' pp. 70–71)

Context
The situation in which an utterance is used. To understand the context you need to have information about the setting, the topic and the roles and relationships of the participants in the interaction. Thus if you wanted information about the context of this utterance: 'There is a two year guarantee but most of our clients find they don't need it', you would need to know where the interaction was taking place (e.g. car showroom), what was being discussed (e.g. an Alfa Romeo Sprint Veloce) and what the roles (e.g. salesman/potential customer), relationship (e.g. strangers) and purposes (e.g. sell a car/find out information) of the participants were.

The context is often referred to as the situational context to differentiate it from the linguistic context (or cotext). However some writers use 'context' to refer to both the situational environment and the linguistic environment (i.e. the other utterances used before and after the one being referred to).

See **Cotext**

Contracted forms
Verb forms which are shortened in informal speech, for example
I've, she's, they'd etc.

Contrastive analysis
Comparing two different languages to discover in what ways they are the same, similar and different in order to predict likely learner errors or explain discovered errors.

See Abbot and Wingard (1981, pp. 229–30)
See **Interference** and **Transfer**

Controlled exercise
A practice exercise in which the learners are told exactly what to do and how to do it. It is hoped that nearly all the learners will get nearly all the exercise right and will therefore develop correct habits and gain useful knowledge about the language.

See Ellis and Tomlinson (1980, pp. 14–15 and pp. 203–206)
(Note Mechanical exercise may be used to mean the same as Controlled exercise)

Correction
The putting right of a particular instance of language use which is considered faulty.
For example,

>Peter his records are many. X
>Peter has a lot of records. ✔

See **Instance** and **Generalisation**
cf. **Remediation**

Cotext
The language which is used before and after a particular utterance being referred to. This is often known as the linguistic environment or the linguistic context of the utterance.
In the example below, the cotext of the utterance, 'If only I'd known,' is in italics

>A *Why the hell did you tell the Director?*
>B If only I'd known. *Nobody told me who he was. I'd have kept quiet if I'd known.*

cf. **Context**

Creation
The ability of a language learner to produce utterances which he has never heard or read and therefore cannot possibly have remembered and reproduced. The learner creates by making use of subconscious generalisations based upon his exposure to the language in use.

See **Generalisation**

Creole
A language which has developed as a result of a combination between local languages and an outside language and which has become the native language of a community of its speakers.

cf. **Pidgin**

Cue cards
(1) Cards shown to learners to guide their responses in a drill.
(2) Cards given to participants in a role-play or simulation to tell them who they are and what they are going to do. *Note* These are sometimes called role cards.

Example:

Salesman
You are a car salesman and you have not sold a car all week. Try to persuade the next person who comes into the showroom to test drive the new XY car.

Cyclical syllabus
A syllabus in which each particular aspect of the language occurs many times. Thus suggestions might be introduced with the pattern '*How about* verb + ing' then four weeks later '*Why don't you* + verb' is presented and then four weeks later both patterns are revised and '*You could try* verb + ing' is presented.

cf. **Linear syllabus**

Declarative
A declarative sentence is one in which the subject precedes its verb. For example:
>Peter collapsed with only a few hundred yards to go.
>(subject) (verb)
One of the main functions of declarative sentences is to make a statement containing

information. However they are also used for such functions as criticism, warning, disagreement, requesting etc. For example:

Excuse me, I'm trying to get to the station.
(request for directions)

cf. **Interrogative** and **Imperative**

Deductive
Referring to the process of consciously working out rules of the language from an analysis of samples of the language.

See **Cognitive approaches**
cf. **Inductive**

Denotation
The actual thing referred to by a word or group of words as opposed to ideas or feelings associated with the word. Thus the denotive meaning of *bow-tie* includes only the normal shape, size, materials etc. of the actual item but does not include its association with formal dress and formal occasions.

Diagnostic test
A test designed to discover what a learner or group of learners can do and cannot do in the language. Such a test would be used at the beginning of a course to provide information on which schemes of work could be based or during a course to provide information relating to a particular area of language scheduled to be taught to the learners.

See Ellis and Tomlinson (1980, pp. 270–274)

Dialect
A variety of a language which differs from its standard form(s) in pronunciation (i.e. accent), in grammar and in vocabulary. Dialects can be regional (e.g. Cockney in the East End of London) or social (e.g. 'Black English' in New York).

See **Varieties**

Dialogue
A conversation presented to the learners to exemplify certain aspects of the spoken language and then used as the basis of practice activities.

See Rivers and Temperley (1978, pp. 24–40)

Dictation
An exercise or test involving the learners writing down the language which is spoken to them. It is claimed that what the learners write reveals evidence about many aspects of their language ability.

See Rivers and Temperley (1978, pp. 269–70)
See **Global tests**

Direct method
An approach to language learning based on induction rather than on deduction and thus on learning the grammar of a language through practice of it rather than through being taught about it.

See **Inductive** and **Deductive**

Discourse
Language used in a real situation for real purposes. In other words language as social behaviour. Such a use of language invariably involves interaction (e.g. between participants in a conversation; between reader and writer in a newspaper article; between lecturer and listeners) and the combining and relating of utterances.

See **Coherence**

Discourse analysis
The study of how a language actually works in real situations. This involves not only studying the phonology, grammar and vocaculary of the language but also the ways in which people interact (e.g. starting a conversation, interrupting, changing the topic, etc.) and the ways in which they use language to achieve situational purposes (e.g. persuading, refusing without giving offence, clarifying information given, etc.)

Discrete point tests
Tests which aim to provide very specific information about learners' abilities in particular skills or in particular language areas (e.g. knowledge of irregular simple past forms). This type of test focuses on one item at a time and therefore tests knowledge of it rather than ability to use it in real situations.

cf. **Communicative tests** and **Global tests**

Drills
Language practice exercises designed to give the learners many opportunities to use the correct forms and thus to establish correct habits. They are designed to demonstrate the regularity of the rule they exemplify and to fix it through repetition in the learner's mind.

See **Behaviourist theories; Inducitve; Meaningful drills** and **Meaningless drills**

EAP (English for Academic Purposes)
EAP courses are designed for students taking or about to take academic courses using English as the medium of instruction. They are usually specially designed to help the participants to understand and use those aspects of English which they will need during their academic courses.

EFL (English as a Foreign Language)
English learned by people from a community where English is not normally used. Thus an Italian, a Russian, an Argentinian or a German learning English would be learning it as a foreign language.

cf. ESL

Elementary level
The lowest of the levels in which EFL learners are placed on entry to a course. Classes at this level include learners ranging from complete beginners to those who have picked up enough English to communicate inaccurately but effectively in everyday situations such as buying a ticket, ordering a meal and buying something from a shop.

EOP (English for Occupational Purposes)
EOP courses are designed for people who need to learn English in order to help them carry out their job. Usually these courses are planned to cater for the specific needs of the participants and thus an EOP course for pilots would be very different from one for hotel managers or customs officials.

Error analysis
Examination of samples of learners' use of English to find out what errors they make and to try to discover evidence indicating the specific nature and causes of the errors.

Errors
Systematic deviations from the norms of the language being learned. They are usually caused by false generalisations about the language by the learner and are an inevitable and essential part of language learning. Many such errors are developmental and disappear as the learner gains more exposure to the language in use.

See **Generalisations** and **Interlanguage**
cf.   **Mistakes**

ESL (English as a Second Language)
English learned by people from communities where English is not the native language but where it is commonly used for various social purposes such as education, commerce, government and religion. Thus an Indian, a Nigerian, a Jamaican, a Fijian or a Kenyan learning English would be learning it as a second language.

cf. EFL

ESP (English for Special Purposes or English for Specific Purposes)
ESP courses are designed for people who are learning English so that they will be able to use it in particular situations such as on a holiday, in their job, in their training or on academic courses.

See EAP and EOP

Examples
Utterances provided by a teacher, a text book, a tape, etc. in order to illustrate specific language points to learners. For example:
> He said, 'They won't bother you again.'
> (an example illustrating the conventions of direct speech).

cf. Instances

Exponents
The actual expressions used to communicate particular aspects of language functions. For example: (function = invitation)
> *Exponents*
> (1) Would you like to come...
> (2) How about coming...
> (3) We'd like you to come...
> (4) We'd be very pleased if you could come...

See Function

Exposure
All the language which the learner hears or reads.

See Input

Extensive reading/listening
Reading or listening to fairly lengthy texts (e.g. a novel, a radio programme) without necessarily achieving a hundred per cent concentration or comprehension.

The main aims are to increase the learners' exposure to language in use, to develop language skills and to stimulate motivation through a sense of enjoyment and achievement.

See Ellis and Tomlinson (1980, pp. 169–70)

False Beginners
Those learners who seem to be complete beginners because of their inability to use the language they are learning but who have had previous learning experiences of the language. They have thus already 'stored' information about the language. This information often becomes activated during the new course and an apparently dramatic improvement takes place. A typical example of a false beginner would be somebody who learned some English whilst at secondary school in his own country but never really used it and then years later came to England to start learning English again.

First language
A person's first language is the one s(he) learned first as a child and which s(he) has continued to use. It is often referred to as L1.

See Mother tongue Native language
cf. Second language

Fluency
The ability to use a language spontaneously and confidently and without undue pauses and hesitations.

Form
An analysis of form would be concerned with such features of expression as pronunciation, spelling, word order, tense formation, grammatical agreement, gender, plurality, etc. It would not be concerned with the meanings these forms are used to convey. For example:

Has he finished his dinner yet?

An analysis of the *form* of the above sentence would describe the subject-verb inversion, the agreement between *he* and *has*, the form of the past participle (*finished*), the form of the present perfect tense, the form of the possessive pronoun (*his*) the position in the sentence of the object (*dinner*) and the position of the adverb (*yet*).

cf. Function

Formulaic expressions
Expressions which are learned as whole utterances (for example, How do you do?) or as patterns which the learner can use by inserting a relevant word in a vacant slot (for example, What does _____ mean?).

Fossilization
Fossilization occurs when a learner's use of the target language ceases to develop and therefore his *errors* become permanent. This usually happens when the learner has attained his or her inner goal (e.g. easy communication in everyday face to face situations) and there is no longer any real motivation for further development.

See Interlanguage   Target language

Function
An analysis of the functions of an utterance would be concerned with its meanings and with the purpose it is being used to achieve. For example:

Don't worry, I go there on Tuesday afternoon.

In the above example the simple present tense (*go*) is used with the function of definite future arrangement and the main *function* of the utterance is probably to reassure somebody that a visit they are suggesting has already been included in an itinerary.

cf. Form

Functional approach
An approach to language teaching which stresses the purposes for which expressions are used. Thus, instead of teaching the structures of English (e.g. the tenses, types of clauses, the passive, etc.) a course based on a functional approach would teach how to express agreement, how to decline an invitation, how to give directions, how to ask for information etc.

See Exponents

Functional syllabus
A syllabus listing which functions and which of their exponents are to be taught. For example:

Disagreement
I'm not sure I agree.
I don't go along with you there.
That's not completely true.   etc.

See Function   Exponents

Generalisations

Assumptions about patterns of the language made by the learner as a result of his exposure to it. For example, many elementary learners make the false generalisation that the past simple tense is always formed by adding –ed to the verb (e.g. *showed*) and thus make such errors as X *buyed* X.

These generalisations are made unconsciously as a result of the brain processing a number of similar utterances.

Making such generalisations is an important part of language learning and is the basis of first language acquisition. The learner revises his generalisations as he receives more 'information' from the language he is exposed to and from reactions to the language he uses himself.

Genuine text

A continuous 'passage' of written or spoken language originally used to achieve real communication but subsequently used in the classroom as a source of exposure to language in use for the learners. Many books use the term *authentic material* with this same meaning.

See Authentic materials   Authentic tasks and Text

Global tests

Tests designed to assess learners' overall language ability rather than to assess particular skills. Cloze tests and dictation tests are the most frequently used global tests.

See Cloze tests
     Dictation

Graded readers

Books written or simplified so as to be suitable for use as extensive reading material for particular levels of learners.

See Extensive reading

Grading

Deciding on the particular order in which you are going to deal with selected teaching points.

Grammar – translation method

A method in which the learner is taught the grammar of the target language and is asked to use the rules he has learned to help him translate from the target language into his native language and vice-versa.

Guided exercises

Practice exercises in which the learners are told what to do and then are given advice on how to do it. The learners have to make some decisions of their own and to create some of their own expressions. For example:

> Write a paragraph saying which towns you have visited since coming to Britain. Remember to use the present perfect when you do not refer to a particular time and the simple past when you do refer to a particular time. e.g. I *have been* to Stratford twice. I *went* there during my first weekend in England and I *went* there again last weekend.

See Ellis and Tomlinson (1980, p. 204 and pp. 206–10)
cf.   Controlled exercise

Humanistic approaches
Approaches to language teaching which stress the importance of treating the learners as individual human beings and require the teacher to be a sympathetic counsellor/guide/friend rather than an authority and instructor.

Illocutionary act
The purpose(s) for which an utterance is made. Thus in the following example John is performing the illocutionary act of inviting and Mary is performing the illocutionary acts of politely declining and justifying.

> John   Would you like to go to the cinema with me tonight?
> Mary   I'm sorry, I can't. I've got a lot of work to do tonight.

See Widdowson (1978, pp. 22–24)
See **Function** and **Discourse**

Imperative
The form of the verb used to give orders, warnings, suggestions, instructions and directions. For example:

> Sit down.
> Look out.
> Do it in rough first.
> Boil for three minutes.
> Turn left.

The imperative is the same form of the verb as the infinitive without *to*.
i.e. infinitive = to stop
     imperative = stop

Inductive
Referring to the process of 'gaining' generalisations about the language as a result of practising sentences which exemplify them.

See **Generalisations** and **Examples**
cf. **Deductive**

Information gap
See **Communication gap**

Input
The language gained from exposure which is available to the brain for language processing.

See **Exposure** and **Intake**

Instances
Utterances used in real discourse.

See **Utterance** and **Discourse**
cf. **Examples**

Intake
The language which the learner unconsciously selects for acquisition from all the language in use he is exposed to.

See **Acquisition** and **Input**

Intensive reading/listening
Reading or listening to a short text with as much concentration and understanding as possible.

See Ellis and Tomlinson (1980, p. 169)
cf. **Extensive reading/listening**

Interaction
Communication between people involving the use of language (e.g. between two people having a conversation, between writer and readers, between speaker and listeners etc.)

See **Discourse**

Interference
The negative influence of one language whilst learning another language. Approximately ten to fifteen percent of L2 errors are caused by such interference – usually as a result of the learner either assuming that similar L1 and L2 patterns are identical or of using familiar (i.e. L1) generalisations when (s)he has not yet formed a relevant L2 generalisation. Most L1 interference errors are either pronunciation or vocabulary errors; very few errors of grammar or syntax are attributable to L1 interference.

See **Generalisations L1 and L2** and **Transfer**

Interlanguage
The language spoken by a learner of a second or foreign language. It is called an interlanguage because it is felt to be in between the learner's first language and the language he is learning. As the learner progresses his interlanguage moves further away from the first language and closer to the language that is being learned. However, the learner still retains features which are peculiar to the interlanguage and which have no apparent connection with the first language or the language he is learning.

See Richards (1978, pp. 72–78)
See **Errors**

Interrogative
The interrogative is used to ask questions seeking information and for such other functions as replying to criticism, (*Have I ever let you down?*) expressing annoyance (*Haven't you finished yet?*) and expressing regret (*Why didn't I listen to him?*).
The form of the interrogative is usually Auxiliary verb + Subject + Verb?
e.g.

Has	he	gone ?
Did	Mary	finish ?
Are	they	coming ?
Why did	you	do it ?

cf. **Declarative** and **Imperative**

Intonation
The rise and fall of the voice used to indicate the function(s) of an utterance. Thus, '*A drink*', said with the voice falling at the end could be the answer to a question whereas if it was said with the voice rising at the end it could be an invitation.

See **Function**

L1
The learner's first language, e.g. English for an Énglishman.

See **EFL Mother tongue** and **Native language**

L2
A language being learned which is not the learner's first language, i.e. a second or foreign language, e.g. English for a Frenchman.

See **EFL ESL**

Language laboratory
A room where learners can listen to and respond to spoken language on tape. Each learner has his or her own tape recorder and earphones and works at his or her own speed.

Language shock
The fear of making errors when using a foreign language. Some learners are so afraid of being humiliated that they are reluctant to use the language at all. Such learners need confidence rather than correction. Role-play, simulation and other communication activities can help by focusing their attention on content and communication rather than expression.

See Communication activities   Role-play   Simulation

Learner-centred approaches
Approaches to language teaching based on the needs and interests of the learners rather than on a fixed syllabus or coursebook and the dictates of a teacher. Such approaches would ideally involve the learners in decisions about what and how they learn and would require the teacher to be an organiser and guide rather than an instructor.

Learning
The process of gaining knowledge about a language as a result of formal instruction by a teacher, conscious effort by the learner and the practice of selected and specific language items and structures.

cf. Acquisition

Lexical item
A word or group of words used in a particular utterance with a specific meaning, for example *wonderful* and *piece of music* in:
        That's a *wonderful piece of music*.

Lexis
Another name for vocabulary (i.e. the words in a language which communicate meaning).

Linear syllabus
A syllabus which is organised and ordered on the principle of adding teaching points to each other one at a time. Most such syllabuses are also progressive syllabuses i.e. learning the first teaching point helps in learning the second teaching point which helps in learning the third, etc.
(For example (1) Personal pronouns; (2) present tense of the verb *to be*; (3) present continuous tense.)

See Synthetic

Lingua franca
A language which is used in an area to facilitate communication between speakers of different languages. For example, in Vanuatu in the south-west Pacific the 100 000 indigenous inhabitants speak 112 different mother tongues and have to use Bislama (a pidgin combining Melanesian structure with English syntax) as a lingua franca to achieve communication with people from different areas of the country.

See Pidgin

Meaningful drills
Practice exercises designed to help the learner to repeat a particular pattern or item many times but which nevertheless require the learner to make choices relating to the meaning of the sentence he produces.

See Dakin (1973, Chapter 5)
See Substitution table and Drills

Meaningless drills
Practice exercises which require no choice and therefore are almost impossible for

the learner to get wrong. In many cases the learner produces correct sentences without having any idea what they mean.

See   Dakin (1973, Chapter 4)
See **Substitution table** and **Drills**
cf.   **Meaningful drills**

Medium of communication
Speech and writing are the basic media of communication.

Medium of instruction
The language in which subjects in an educational institution are taught. For example,
English is the medium of instruction in Nigerian secondary schools.

Mistakes
Deviations from the norms of a language caused by such non-linguistic factors as
carelessness, tiredness, boredom, excitement, tension etc.

cf.   **Errors**

Modal verbs
Verbs which add to the meaning of the main verb. They usually indicate the attitude of
the speaker or writer. For example:

> They *should* win.
> He *ought to* visit his father.
> She *will* pass the exam.

See   **Auxiliary verbs**

Monitoring
The process of assessing the accuracy, appropriateness and effectiveness of your
own utterances. In learning a second language it is very important to achieve the right
amount of monitoring. Those learners who under-monitor usually achieve communication without correctness and those who over-monitor produce very correct utterances but are too worried about making errors to be fluent.

See Krashen (1981, pp. 12–13)
See   **Fluency**

Morphology
When we talk about the morphology of a word we are referring to the bits which make
up the word. Thus we might divide up the word *postponement* into three bits as
follows:

1 *post* = a prefix meaning after
2 *pone* = the root of the word meaning *putting, placing* or *arranging*
3 *ment* = a suffix indicating that the word is a noun.

Mother tongue
The language learned by the child from his parents and peers.

See **First language** and **Native language**

Multilingual
A person who can use many languages.

Multiple choice
Exercises and tests requiring the learners to select the correct answer from a number
of possible answers. For example:

> Last week they _____ to Paris and then went by train to Nice.
> (a) have flown   (b) fly
> (c) flew   (d) had flown
> (e) were flying

Native language
The language learned as a child because it is the one used in the child's environment.

See **First language** and **Mother tongue**

Native speaker
A person who speaks a language as his first language (i.e. as the language he first learned as a child).

Notion
A concept (or area of meaning) such as time, duration, quantity or space.

See Wilkins (1976, p. 24 and pp. 25–55)

Notional approach
An approach to language teaching which concentrates on teaching the learners how to express different aspects of the main concepts represented by the language (e.g. ways of referring to the future, to quantity, to time, to duration, to space, to quality, etc.)

See **Notional syllabus**

Notional syllabus
A language teaching syllabus which concentrates on teaching points which are ways of expressing different aspects of the main concepts communicated by the language. e.g. *Quantity*

some	a few
any	a little
all	half
both	a lot
etc.	etc.

See Wilkins (1976, pp. 18–20) Van Ek (1977, pp. 39–42)
See **Notional approach**

Objective test
A test which has a limited, predictable and definite number of possible answers and therefore only requires the marker(s) to follow a marking key.

See Heaton (1975, pp. 11–14)

Objectives
Statements of what the learners should be able to do in the language by a certain point. For example:

> By the end of the course the learners should be able to note down the main points of a first year university lecture on Economics.

> By the end of Week Four the learners should be able to order a meal in a restaurant and get what they want without causing problems for the waiter or themselves.

Ideally objectives should be measurable and stated in terms of target-language behaviour.

Ostensive definition
A way of demonstrating the meaning of a word or group of words by getting the learners to experience the meaning through their senses. For example:

> feeling material which is *rough*,
> hearing a *scream*,
> smelling something which is *fragrant*,
> tasting something *sour*,
> seeing a picture of a *helicopter*.

See Ellis and Tomlinson (1980, pp. 67–68)

Output
The learner's output is the language he uses himself.

cf. Input   Intake

Overgeneralisation
A generalisation made by the learner which fails to take account of exceptions and which therefore covers too large an area of the language. For example:

      (a) the overgeneralisation that the verb in the present simple tense is always the same as the infinitive without *to* (∴ X 'He live in London'X)

      (b) the overgeneralisation that the present continuous tense is always used when you want to refer to 'now' (∴X 'I am seeing a mountain'X)

See Bolitho and Tomlinson (1980)
See **Generalisation**

Paradigmatic
This refers to the vertical choices speakers of a language have in every utterance they make. For example:

1	2		3
She Mary My sister	hates dislikes loathes	being	interrogated. questioned. asked.

The speaker selects the most appropriate item to fill the slots 1, 2 and 3.

Cf. **Syntagmatic**

Participants
People taking part in an interaction (e.g. a speaker and the audience, people having a conversation, a writer and readers).

See **Interaction** and **Discourse**

Pidgin
A language evolved as a result of contact between two different languages (or language families) usually to facilitate trade (e.g. Pidgin English in Papua New Guinea), the spreading of religion or ideas (e.g. Pidgin English in Nigeria and Vanuatu) or the carrying out of a particular project (e.g. Pidgin American in Vietnam).

Usually the new language bases its structure on the 'host' language(s) and its vocabulary on the 'visiting' language, but then very often develops features peculiar to itself.

See Todd (1974)

cf. **Creole**

Pidginization
The process of two or more languages mixing together to form one language capable of achieving communication.

Practice
Exercises, activities, drills, etc. designed to give the learners opportunities to produce correct sentences which include particular language items or structures they have recently been taught.

Presentation
The stage of a lesson when the teacher actively teaches particular language points through demonstration, exemplification, explanation, description, definition, etc.

Progressive syllabus
See Linear syllabus

Production
(1) The use of language.
(2) The section of a lesson or unit requiring the learners to use particular language skills or items. Usually production comes after presentation and practice of the teaching point but in some 'modern' approaches production comes first and then the teacher decides what to present and practise.

See Analytical   Presentation   Practice and Synthetic

Productive skills
Speaking and writing (i.e. those skills requiring production of language).

cf. Receptive skills

Realia
Objects from real life used in the language classroom as aids (e.g. a real menu, a table cloth, knives and forks, etc. for a practice activity based on ordering food in a restaurant).

Receptive skills
Listening and reading (i.e. those skills requiring the ability to receive communication but not to produce it). These skills used to be referred to as *passive* skills.

Recycling
The frequent repeating of a teaching point (usually focusing on different aspects each time). For example:

Teaching Point = Disagreement
Week 1 – (1) *I don't agree* (2) *I don't think I agree with you*
Week 3 – (1) + (2) + (3) *Are you sure*?
Week 5 – (1) + (2) + (3) + (4) *I have doubts about that.*

Redundancy
Approximately 50 per cent of all items in a spoken English utterance are redundant (i.e. they are not absolutely vital in order to achieve communication). Such redundancy is very important as it helps to ensure that communication takes place even if the participants do not hear and understand everything that is said. For example, the words in italics in this sentence are not all essential: He then *asked* the *question*, 'Where *did you* put it?'

Referent
The referent of a word is the actual object, idea, emotion, etc. it refers to.

See Ellis and Tomlinson (1980, p. 67)

Register
The language appropriate to particular types of situations (e.g. the register of the church, the register of the law court, the register of informal pub conversation, the register of a debate, etc.)

Remedial card
A card designed to help learners to remedy a particular error. Side one of the card contains teaching material and side two practice and testing material. The learner reads the examples, corrections, explanations, etc. on side one and then turns over the card and does the exercises on side two.

Remedial cards enable the teacher to provide each learner with remedial work relevant to his or her discovered problems.

See Ellis and Tomlinson (1980, pp. 283–285) (*Note* Remedial cards are referred to as correction cards)

Remediation
The gradual 'putting right' of a learner's false generalisation about an aspect of a language through increasing his exposure to and monitored use of that particular aspect and thus getting the learner to revise his generalisation.

See Ellis and Tomlinson (1980, pp. 277–285)
cf. Correction

Role cards
See Cue cards 2

Role-play activities
Activities in which the learners play parts (e.g. waiter, customer, policeman, wife, etc.) and practise language appropriate to the situations they are placed in (e.g. a customer ordering a meal in a restaurant). In this way the learners often lose some of their inhibitions and are usually less frightened of making mistakes.

cf. Simulation

Rules
(1) Statements about normal language behaviour given to learners by grammar books, text books and teachers in the hope that they will help them to produce correct English.
(2) Statements about the norms of a language. For example: '*Some* is generally used in affirmative sentences; *any* is used in interrogative and negative sentences.'

Such rules are convenient for describing the language but are rarely absolutely true.

Scheme of work
A plan of what a teacher intends to do with a particular group of learners over a particular period of time.

cf. Syllabus

Second language (L2)
A language learned after the mother tongue has been acquired.

See L2

Setting
The location in which an interaction is taking place (e.g. restaurant, office, pub, shop).

Silent way
A method of language teaching in which the teacher remains as silent as possible and elicits responses from the learners by using charts, rods (coloured blocks of wood) and gestures.

See Rivers and Temperly (1978, pp. 19–20).

Simulation
An attempt to create a 'real' situation in the classroom with a setting, a topic, participants and situational purposes. For example:

setting	courtroom
topic	motives for killing a particular person
participants	judge, barristers, the accused, witnesses
purposes	establish truth, prove guilty, prove innocent, etc.

cf. **Role play**

Situational composition
An exercise which provides the learners with information about why they are writing and who they are writing to and then requires them to produce a piece of writing

designed to achieve the situational purposes specified (e.g. writing a letter to a particular personality asking him to attend a particular function at the school).

See Ellis and Tomlinson (1980)
See Tomlinson (1981)

Situational syllabus
An EFL syllabus based on lists of situations the learners are likely to have to use English in (e.g. the Restaurant, the Station, Hotels, the Bank, the Hospital, etc.).

Situational teaching
Approaches to teaching EFL which use the creation of 'real' situations in the classroom (e.g. a doctor examining a patient) in order to exemplify particular aspects of language use and to provide meaningful opportunities for the practice and use of language items.

Speech act
Doing something through language (e.g. getting something repaired, getting help, arranging a meeting).

See Wilkins (1976, pp. 40–45).
See **Discourse   Functions** and **Illocutionary act.**

Stress
The saying of particular sounds with greater force than others. For example:
_quick_ly
_walk_ing
He _gave_ the _book_ to her.
I _want_ed a _red_ one.

See Ellis and Tomlinson (1980, pp. 103–104).

Structural approach
An approach to EFL teaching based on the presentation and practice of the basic structures of the language. In other words, the learners are taught the grammar of the language.

Structural syllabus
A syllabus based on a list of structures to be taught (e.g. the Present Perfect Tense, Reported Speech, Question Tags).

Style
(1) The particular way an author expresses himself.
(2) The type of expression appropriate to particular purposes and situations.

Subjective test
A test which requires the markers to evaluate and not just to follow a mark sheet (e.g. a test involving essay answers).

See Heaton (1975, p. 11).
cf. **Objective test**

Substitution table
A means of providing practice of correct structures. The learner selects from columns and then combines the elements he has chosen in order to make a sentence.
Example (1)

Mary	likes	eating ice-cream.
She	loves	drinking beer.
He	hates	reading books
Bill	dislikes	doing homework.

e.g. *She hates drinking beer.*

Example (2)

Bill	were pleased	that a few people helped
They	was angry	that little work was done.
Mary	was delighted	that few pupils passed the exam.
The teachers	were disappointed	that a little profit was made.

e.g. *Bill was delighted that a little profit was made.*

Note In (1) the learner can combine any of the elements and make a correct and sensible sentence. However, in (2) the learner must decide which elements combine correctly and sensibly. (1) is a meaningless drill whereas (2) is a meaningful drill.

See **Meaningful drills** and **Meaningless drills**

Suggestopedia
A humanistic teaching method which tries to make the learning as relaxed and comfortable as possible (e.g. armchairs, soft music, pleasant colours, etc.) and to make maximum use of the brain's capacity to combine the conscious and the unconscious for learning.

Survival English
The English needed by overseas visitors to an English-speaking area in order to manage such everyday activities as buying goods, ordering meals, cashing cheques, booking accommodation, travelling by public transport etc.

Syllabus
A document outlining the main teaching points to be taught to a particular type of group of learners in a particular institution or group of institutions. Many syllabuses also order the teaching points, many specify objectives and some suggest activities, materials and methods.

cf. **Scheme of work**

Syntagmatic
Relating to the choices a user of a language has to make in order to relate one item in an utterance to the other items already selected. For example:

I spoke to the
{
woman. ✔
her. x
Mary. x
boys. ✔
telephone. x
}

cf. **Paradigmatic**

Syntax
The grammatical arrangement of words in an utterance. Rules of syntax thus deal with permissable combinations, word orders and obligatory agreements.

Synthetic
A synthetic approach is one which teaches items one by one and which restricts the learner to those items he has already been taught plus a few new item(s) in each lesson.

Cf. **Analytical**

Target language (TL)
The language the learner is trying to learn. Thus English is the target language for any overseas student learning English as a second or foreign language.

Teaching points

Particular aspects of the language selected by the teacher for presentation to a particular class of learners.

TEFL

Teaching English as a foreign language.

See EFL

Text

A continuous 'piece' of written or spoken language.

See **Discourse**

Theme

A particular subject used as the basis of a unit of teaching. (e.g. Famous People, Justice, Music).

See **Topic**

Topic

(1) What is being talked about in a particular situation.
(2) A particular theme used as the basis of a unit of teaching (e.g. Sport, Hotels, Medicine).

See **Theme**

Transfer

(1) The influence of one language during the acquisition of another language.
(2) The use of skills, etc. developed in association with one language whilst using another language.

See **Interference**

Usage

Language performance in artificial practice situations such as drills, exercises, multiple choice tests, etc. In such situations the learner is really producing evidence of his knowledge of the language rather than of his ability to use it in situations outside the classroom.

See Widdowson (1978, Chapter 1)
cf. **Use**

Use

Language performance in situations which have genuine communicative purposes and are not designed just to practise particular language items or structures. Thus a learner who is having a discussion in a pub or is asking a classmate to lend him a pen is actually using the language.

See Widdowson (1978, Chapter 1)
See **Acquisition**
cf. **Usage**

Utterance

Any complete unit of language used for communicative purpose. An utterance can be either written or spoken. Examples:

> *Put the* (not an utterance because not complete)
> *Smoke*? (an utterance)
> *I like roses, don't you*? (an utterance)
> *I'm going...going there...to London that is...tomor...on Tuesday* (an utterance)
> *The dog bit the man. The man was bitten by the dog.* (not an utterance because not used for a communicative purpose).

Varieties
(1) Different types of language used in different types of situations.
(2) Different regional versions of a language (e.g. American English, Nigerian English, Irish English, Indian English etc.).

Visual Aid
Teaching aid designed to give a visual stimulus, act as a visual prompt or provide visual reinforcement for language items being learned. Photos, cartoons, film strips, blackboard drawings, puppets and wall pictures can be used as visual aids.

See **Audio-visual aids**

Bibliography

Abbot, G. and Wingard, P. (1981), *The Teaching of English as an Inter-national Language* (London: Collins)

Abbs, B., Ayton, A. & Freebairn, I. (1975a), *Strategies* (London: Longman)

Abbs, B., Ayton, A. & Freebairn, I. (1975b), *Strategies Teacher's Book* (London: Longman)

Abbs, B. and Freebairn, I. (1977), *Starting Strategies Students' Book* (London: Longman)

Abbs, B. and Freebairn, I. (1979), *Building Strategies* (London: Longman)

Alexander, L. G. (1967a), *First Things First* (London: Longman)

Alexander, L. G. (1967b), *Practice and Progress* (London: Longman)

Baker, A. (1977), *Ship or Sheep*? (Cambridge: CUP)

Barnett, J. A. (1968), *Success with English: Tapescripts 1* (Harmondsworth:Penguin)

Beijing Languages Institute (1979) *English 1.*

Benhamou, E. and Dominique, P. (1972), *Speak English – class de sixième* (Paris: Nathan)

Bolitho, R. and Tomlinson, B. (1980), *Discover English* (London: Heinemann Educational)

Broughton, G. (1969), *Success with English: Coursebook 2* (Harmondsworth: Penguin)

Brumfit, C. (1977), 'Commonsense about ESP' in Holden, S. (ed.) *English for Specific Purposes* (London: Modern English Publications)

Buckby, M. (1981), 'Graded objectives and tests for modern languages: an evaluation', *British Journal of Language Teaching*, 19:1, Spring 1981.

Byrne, D. (1977), 'Cuecards for interaction', *Modern English Teacher* 5:3, September 1977.

Byrne, D. (1979), *Teaching Writing Skills* (London: Longman)

Cazden, C. B. (1970), 'The situation: a neglected source of social class differences in language use' in Pride J. B. and Holmes, J. (eds.) (1972), *Sociolinguistics* (Harmondsworth: Penguin)

Cook, V. J. (1979), *Using Intonation* (London: Longman)

Cooper, J. (1979), *Think and Link* (London: Edward Arnold)

Cunningsworth, A. J. (1979), 'The London Transport Project' in Sion, C. (ed.) *Recipe Book for Tired Teachers No. 1* (Canterbury: Pilgrims Publications)

Dakin, J. (1973), *The Language Laboratory and Language Learning* (London: Longman)

Ellis, R. and Tomlinson, B. (1980), *Teaching Secondary English* (London: Longman)

Freebairn, I. (1977), *Starting Strategies – Teacher's Book* (London: Longman)

de Freitas, J. F. (1978), *Survival English* (London: Macmillan)

Garton-Sprenger, J. *et al* (1979), *Encounters* (London: Heinemann Educational Books)

Gattegno, C. (1976), *The Common Sense of Teaching Foreign Languages* (New York: Educational Solutions)

Granger, C. and Hicks, T. (1977), *Contact English* (London: Heinemann Educational Books)

Hartley, B. and Viney, P. (1978), *Streamline English Departures – Teacher's Edition* (Oxford: OUP)

Heaton, J. B. (1975), *Writing English Language Tests* (London: Longman)

Hymes, D.H. (1971), 'On communicative competence' in Pride, J.B. and Holmes, J. (ed.) (1972), *Sociolinguistics* (Harmondsworth: Penguin)

Krashen, S. (1981), *Second Language Acquisition and Second Language Learning* (Oxford: Pergamon)

Longman (1968), Longman Structural Readers Handbook

Longman (1977), Longman Guide to Graded Reading

Milne, J. (1977), *Heinemann Guided Readers Handbook* (London: Heinemann Educational Books)

Mortimer, C. (1975), *Sound Right!* (London: Longman)

Mortimer, C. (1976), *Stress Time* (Cambridge: CUP)

Moskowitz, G. (1978), *Caring and Sharing in the Foreign Language Class* (Rowley, Mass.: Newbury House)

Nicholls, S. *et al* (1977), *English Alive 1* (London: Edward Arnold)

O'Neill, R. (1973), *Kernel Lessons Plus* (London: Longman)

O'Neill, R. (1979), *Kernel One – Teacher's Book* (London: Longman)

Oxford University Press (1979), *Reading and Thinking in English – Discovering Discourse*

Quirk, R. *et al* (1972), *A Grammar of Contemporary English* (London: Longman)

Quirk, R. and Greenbaum S. (1973), *A University Grammar of English.* (London: Longman)

Richards, J.C. (1976), 'The role of vocabulary teaching', *TESOL Quarterly* 10:1, March 1976, pp. 77–89.

Richards, J.C. (1978), *Understanding Second and Foreign Language Learning* (Rowley, Mass.: Newbury House)

Rivers, W.M. (1968), *Teaching Foreign-Language Skills* (Chicago: University of Chicago Press)

Rivers, W.M. and Temperley, M.S. (1978), *A Practical Guide to the Teaching of English* (Oxford: OUP)

Robinson, P. (1980), *ESP (English for Specific Purposes)* (Oxford: Pergamon)

Spencer, D.H. (1967), *Guided Composition Exercises* (London: Longman)

Stevick, E.W. (1976), *Memory Meaning & Method* (Rowley, Mass: Newbury House)

Stevick, E.W. (1980), *A Way and Ways* (Rowley, Mass.: Newbury House)

Stubbs, M. (1980), *Language and Literacy* (London: Routledge and Kegan Paul)

Thomson, A.J. and Martinet, A.V. (1961), *A Practical English Grammar – Exercises 1: Present and Past Tenses* (Oxford: OUP)

Todd, L. (1974), *Pidgins and Creoles* (London: Routledge and Kegan Paul)

Tomlinson, B. (1981), *O-Level Summary and Composition* (London: Longman)

Van Ek, J.A. (1977), *The Threshold Level for Modern Language Learning in Schools* (London: Longman)

Watcyn-Jones, P. (1981), *Pair Work* (Harmondsworth: Penguin)

Widdowson, H.G. (1978), *Teaching Language as Communication* (Oxford: OUP)

Widdowson, H.G. (1979), *Explorations in Applied Linguistics* (Oxford: OUP)

Wilkins, D.A. (1976), *Notional Syllabuses* (Oxford: OUP)

Index

Other Heinemann titles for teachers and trainee teachers of English include:

Practical Language Teaching Series

Editors: Marion Geddes and Gill Sturtridge

PLT 1 *Planning and Using the Blackboard*
Patricia Mugglestone

PLT 2 *Using the Magnetboard*
Donn Byrne

PLT 3 *The Magazine Picture Library*
Janet McAlpin

PLT 4 *Teaching Written English*
Ron White

PLT 5 *Using Blackboard Drawing*
Peter Shaw and Thérèse de Vet

PLT 6 *Photographic Slides in Language Teaching*
Angela Ayton and Margaret Morgan

PLT 7 *Video in the Language Classroom*
Edited by Marion Geddes and Gill Sturtridge

PLT 8 *Using the Overhead Projector*
J. R. H. Jones

PLT 9 *Teaching Reading Skills in a Foreign Language*
Christine Nuttall

PLT 10 *Teaching Vocabulary*
Michael Wallace

Sourcebooks

Discover English
Rod Bolitho and Brian Tomlinson

Towards the Creative Teaching of English
Langenheim, Melville, Rinvolucri and Spaventa

Source Book for Teaching English Overseas
Michael Lewis and Jimmie Hill

Teaching Practice Handbook
Roger Gower and Steve Walters